BET BUSES
in the 1960s

Gavin Booth

Ian Allan
PUBLISHING

Front cover: Many of the BET companies operated in industrial areas where big buses were needed to move the passengers, and some required lowheight buses that could pass under low railway bridges. East Midland, with many works and colliery services, standardised on lower-height buses for its double-deck fleet, including Leyland Titans with lowbridge bodies and Leyland-Albion Lowlander LR7s with Alexander bodies, like this 1962 example. *Mark Page*

Back cover, upper: More than half of the BET fleets in the 1960s carried red liveries, so the dark blue and primrose of the East Yorkshire company was particularly distinctive. This 1955 Leyland Titan PD2/12, seen in Hornsea in 1963, carries a lowbridge 56-seat Park Royal body. Leyland and Park Royal were mainstream suppliers to BET fleets. *Martin Llewellyn/Omnicolour*

Back cover, lower: Neither Daimler nor Alexander were major BET suppliers at the start of the 1960s, but as BET moved through its final decade operating buses in England and Wales, Daimler's Fleetline chassis and Alexander's stylish bodies became more familiar. Potteries bought 25 of these Fleetline CRG6LX with lowheight Alexander D-type 72-seat bodies in 1964. This one is seen in Hanley when new. *Martin Llewellyn/Omnicolour*

PAGE 1: Photographed when new, right in the middle of the 1960s, a 1965 Devon General AEC Regent V 2D3RA with 69-seat Park Royal forward entrance body, represents two of BET's major suppliers as well as a type of bus that was out of favour in some BET fleets as they turned to the new rear-engined Leyland Atlantean and Daimler Fleetline double-deckers and high-capacity single-deckers. *Royston Morgan*

First published 2011

ISBN 978 0 7110 3464 8

© Ian Allan Publishing 2011

Published by Ian Allan Publishing

an imprint of Ian Allan Publishing Ltd, Hersham, Surrey, KT12 4RG

Printed by Ian Allan Printing Ltd, Hersham, Surrey, KT12 4RG

Code: 1107/B2

Visit the Ian Allan website at www.ianallanpublishing.com

Contents

Many of the photographs for this book were supplied by an old friend, Mark Page, who sadly died before the book was published. This book is dedicated to his memory.

Introduction

BET buses belong to that rather more innocent and slow-moving Britain of at least 40 years ago, when buses in England and Wales fell into obvious camps – the big company fleets, represented by the BET and Tilling groups, the municipal fleets, some 90 of them at the time, and of course the independents, typically small- to medium-sized, but with some major players like Barton Transport, Lancashire United and West Riding.

That was the situation in 1960, the start of the period covered by this book, yet during the 1960s the bus world would change dramatically. Against the background of impending legislation that would change the face of bus operation, the once proudly independent BET Group decided to sell its UK bus interests to the state – represented by the Transport Holding Company (THC) – setting the scene for a single massive state-controlled bus giant, the National Bus Company.

BET's decision to sell was no doubt prompted by a number of factors, not least that it was becoming more difficult to run a bus business profitably against the background of passenger numbers that had been falling dramatically since the golden days of the early post-Second World War years. BET had fought against state control at the time the railways were nationalised, while the Tilling and Scottish groups, with substantial railway shareholdings, decided to sell to the state. BET companies also had railway shareholdings, but the group had managed to stay in private hands.

Well into the 1960s it was 'business as usual' for Britain's bus operators, who were often simply managing decline rather than looking at innovative ways to stem the fall in passenger numbers. But then in the late 1960s there were strong indications of a more centralist approach to running buses, not only with the creation of a National Bus Company, but also with proposals to create Passenger Transport Executives in four of England's largest conurbations, and the implied threat to many of the most profitable routes operated by BET companies. Added to this, BET's portfolio had long since diversified into a range of new businesses, and running buses for minimal profits suddenly seemed less attractive.

So, after years of BET buses operated through a network of very individualistic companies, the sale to THC was the first step on a road towards a more corporate approach that would lose much of the individuality and result in there being little to distinguish buses in one part of England and Wales from another.

The photos in this book illustrate the world in which BET operated in the 1960s – often empty roads, rarely anything but British-built cars, and a surprising number of buses carrying adverts for alcoholic drinks. Very different from the electronic, low-floor, broadband, Euro 5, iPod, *X Factor*, corporate image world of the 21st century!

Half a century on from 1960, the bus scene has changed beyond recognition, but the foundations laid by the BET companies are still there to see in many of today's bus routes. BET was good at recognising where the passengers were and where they wanted to travel. That was the secret of its success over the years and this book is a tribute to the far-sightedness of BET managers and their determination to run good profitable businesses.

Gavin Booth
Edinburgh
June 2011

RIGHT: The 36-foot-long single-decker quickly became a BET Group staple, with bodywork to this distinctive style – built by a number of companies – on AEC Reliance or Leyland Leopard chassis. This Trent Leopard PSU3/1R with Willowbrook 49-seat body was new in 1965. *Royston Morgan*

1 | Background to BET

The British Electric Traction Group was a significant force in the bus industry in England and Wales in the 1960s. It operated some 11,000 buses and coaches through a network of more than 30 subsidiary companies and was marginally larger in terms of fleet size than the other major bus group of the time, the state-owned Tilling Group, which ran some 10,500 buses through roundly 30 subsidiaries in England and Wales, and there were a further 4,600 in the state-owned Scottish Bus Group.

Although BET had some history in Scotland, by the 1960s it was concentrating on its bus interests in England and Wales, and BET and Tilling between them controlled a substantial proportion of the territorial bus operations; there were also corporation fleets in 91 towns and cities, and a few

significant independent operators like Barton, Lancashire United and West Riding.

The map shows that BET influence was strong in North West and North East England, in Yorkshire, through the Midlands to Oxfordshire, and in South Wales and South East England. Although Tilling fleets like Crosville, Eastern Counties, Lincolnshire, Southern and Western National and United Auto all served large areas, there was much deeply rural territory, which compared with the very compact urban operations of BET fleets like Northern General, Potteries, Trent, Yorkshire Traction and Yorkshire Woollen.

In a way this reflected BET's roots. The British Electric Traction name tells us that BET started in the late 19th century, in 1895, in the years before motorbuses when electric

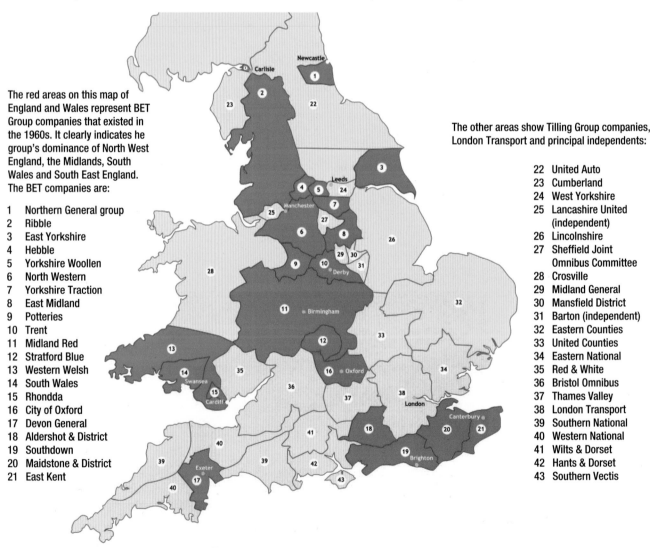

The red areas on this map of England and Wales represent BET Group companies that existed in the 1960s. It clearly indicates he group's dominance of North West England, the Midlands, South Wales and South East England. The BET companies are:

1 Northern General group
2 Ribble
3 East Yorkshire
4 Hebble
5 Yorkshire Woollen
6 North Western
7 Yorkshire Traction
8 East Midland
9 Potteries
10 Trent
11 Midland Red
12 Stratford Blue
13 Western Welsh
14 South Wales
15 Rhondda
16 City of Oxford
17 Devon General
18 Aldershot & District
19 Southdown
20 Maidstone & District
21 East Kent

The other areas show Tilling Group companies, London Transport and principal independents:

22 United Auto
23 Cumberland
24 West Yorkshire
25 Lancashire United (independent)
26 Lincolnshire
27 Sheffield Joint Omnibus Committee
28 Crosville
29 Midland General
30 Mansfield District
31 Barton (independent)
32 Eastern Counties
33 United Counties
34 Eastern National
35 Red & White
36 Bristol Omnibus
37 Thames Valley
38 London Transport
39 Southern National
40 Western National
41 Wilts & Dorset
42 Hants & Dorset
43 Southern Vectis

tramcars were the latest thing in local transport. BET's policy was to acquire an interest in as many of the existing horse and steam tramways with a view to electrifying them – operating the trams and supplying electricity. Local authorities were required to lease operation of their local tramway systems to outside companies, usually for 21 years, after which the municipality could operate trams directly, or could sell the undertaking. BET became the largest of the groups set up to operate electric tramways, and by 1906 was responsible for operating 15% of the tramways in the UK – from the island of Bute in Scotland to Kent in South East England. The standard work, *Great British Tramway Networks*, lists the tramways that were electrified and extended under BET control. Some passed to operators outside the BET Group and some passed into municipal ownership at the time of compulsory purchase, but the tramways that survived in the group and were the foundations of BET's bus empire were those at Barnsley, Gateshead, Mumbles, Potteries, Swansea, Tynemouth and Yorkshire Woollen. The BET tramways at Birmingham & Midland, Dudley and Stourbridge, Gravesend, Jarrow, Kidderminster, North Staffs and South Staffs were sold to other companies in the BET Group.

Second in size to BET was the National Electric Construction company (NEC), with tramways at Mexborough, Oxford, Rhondda and Torquay, which were the foundations of the bus companies that passed into BET hands when NEC was acquired in 1931.

BET quickly recognised the potential of the new motorbuses that were appearing in the early 20th century, sometimes as feeders to its tramway networks, and sometimes for services in their own right. As early as 1902 BET had set up an automobile committee, and this was formalised as British Automobile Development Ltd (BAD) in 1905, renamed British Automobile Traction Co Ltd (BAT) in 1912.

At the same time as BET was developing its tramway and bus interests, another important player was emerging. Thomas Tilling had recognised the potential of horsebuses and motorbuses in London, but the strength of the new London General company restricted Tilling's growth there and it started looking for opportunities elsewhere. BET and Tilling found themselves with motorbus operations in Kent and combined to set up the East Kent company. But Tilling also held a substantial stake in BAT and, with BET, set up Tilling & British Automobile Traction Ltd (T&BAT) in 1928, which helped to expand the Tilling portfolio.

This was a time of major change for the bus industry. Motorbuses were now much more refined and reliable vehicles, and their use was spreading rapidly throughout the UK. The four main-line railway companies – Great Western Railway (GWR), London Midland & Scottish Railway (LMS), London & North Eastern Railway (LNER) and Southern Railway (SR) – were watching the growth of bus travel with some concern and obtained parliamentary powers to operate passenger and goods road vehicles. Some railway companies, notably the GWR, already ran bus services, but instead of direct operation they generally chose to buy into the emerging territorial companies. In some cases they bought bus companies, and in others they formed joint operating committees with some of the Yorkshire municipal undertakings. BET companies with no railway shareholdings were Potteries and South Wales Transport.

T&BAT companies in the 1930s included Aldershot & District, Bristol Tramways, Crosville, Cumberland, East Kent, East Midland, East Yorkshire, Eastern Counties,

LEFT: Yorkshire Traction's roots were in the Barnsley & District Electric Traction company, formed in 1902 by BET to operate trams around Barnsley. The company started running buses in 1913, rapidly expanding to replace the trams in 1930 – after renaming the company Yorkshire Traction two years earlier. This 1962 Leyland Titan PD3A/1 with a 73-seat Northern Counties body is leaving Doncaster for the company's home town of Barnsley.
Stewart J. Brown

LEFT: BET formed the Potteries Electric Traction company in 1898 to operate electric trams, and bus services started in earnest in 1913. The last trams ran in 1928 and in 1933 the company was renamed Potteries Motor Traction. This is a 1956 PMT Daimler CVG5 with Northern Counties 59-seat lowbridge bodywork at Longton in 1965.
Martin Llewellyn/Omnicolour

Hants & Dorset, Lincolnshire, Maidstone & District, North Western, Ribble, Southdown, Southern Vectis, Thames Valley, Trent, United Auto, West Yorkshire, Wilts & Dorset and Yorkshire Traction. BET retained direct control of others, typically those that had begun as tramway companies.

By 1942 the T&BAT situation was unravelled and its interests were shared between BET Omnibus Services Ltd and Tilling Motor Services Ltd. Tilling chose largely rural operations while BET mainly took the more compact urban operations. So BET took Aldershot & District, East Kent, East Midland, East Yorkshire, Maidstone & District, North Western, Ribble, Southdown, Trent and Yorkshire Traction; most were the obvious choices, though East Midland and North Western might have been expected to go to Tilling. On the other hand Tilling took Crosville, Cumberland, Eastern Countries, Hants & Dorset, Lincolnshire, Southern Vectis, Thames Valley, United Auto, West Yorkshire and Wilts & Dorset; the surprises here were Crosville, Cumberland and Lincolnshire, which might have been expected to stay with BET. In addition, BET had the companies that had remained firmly in its control, typically the former tramway and ex-NEC companies – Devon General, Hebble, Mexborough & Swinton, Midland Red, Northern General, City of Oxford, Rhondda, Western Welsh and Yorkshire Woollen.

With railway shareholdings in most BET companies, the prospect of compulsory state ownership loomed. Tilling, together with the SMT group, opted for state ownership; in most cases the Government already owned half of the share capital in these companies following the nationalisation of the railways in 1948, and the new British Transport Commission (BTC) would probably have been happy to see BET follow suit. But BET had other ideas and became a vocal opponent of state ownership.

The accompanying 'Timeline' panel shows how BET grew and how its 1960s bus and coach operations came to be part of the group. They continued to make a valuable contribution to BET's profits for most of the 1960s, but once again the world was changing and the directors of BET evidently felt that enough was enough. The resulting sale of BET's UK bus interests to the Transport Holding Company paved the way for a National Bus Company that lived up to its name – well, in England and Wales anyway. At the time of the creation of NBC, former BET companies contributed marginally more than half of the giant new 20,000-strong fleet.

At an early stage in its history BET had moved into the direct relay of broadcast material by setting up the Rediffusion business, and with the nationalisation of the electricity supply companies it had recognised the need to diversify in the UK and overseas. It became involved in the Associated-Rediffusion television franchise, and diversified further into areas like air-conditioning, laundry, office management, waste disposal, background music, publishing, telecommunications, burglar alarms, aircraft flight simulators and CCTV systems. In 1956 BET acquired a 20% interest in the United Transport company, the rump of the old Red & White business, and United Transport became a wholly owned subsidiary of BET in 1971.

In 1987 BET briefly re-entered the UK bus market, when United Transport formed the Bee Line Buzz Company to operate minibus services in the Manchester area, and started a similar operation in Preston under the Zippy name. However, in 1988 United sold Bee Line and Zippy to Ribble, which of course had been formerly owned by BET.

In the meantime BET had recognised that its businesses had become too diverse and sold many off, remaining in facilities management. The company was renamed BET plc in 1985, and was acquired by Rentokil in 1996.

BET timeline

1895	British Electric Traction (Pioneer) Co Ltd set up
1896	British Electric Traction Ltd set up
1897	Gateshead & District trams bought by BET
	Tynemouth & District trams bought by BET
1898	BET forms Potteries Electric Traction company
1902	BET forms automobile committee
	BET forms Barnsley & District company (later Yorkshire Traction)
1903	Yorkshire Woollen formed by BET
1904	Birmingham & Midland Motor Omnibus company formed
1905	BET forms British Automobile Development Co Ltd
1907	NEC starts Mexborough & Swinton trams
1911	Maidstone & District formed, later a BAT interest
1912	BET forms British Automobile Traction Co Ltd
	Aldershot & District formed by BAT
1913	Northern General formed by BET
	Trent formed by BAT and Commercial Car Hirers Ltd
	North Western Road Car company formed by BAT and Tilling
1914	South Wales Transport formed by BET
1915	Southdown formed with BET and Tilling interests
1916	East Kent formed with BET and Tilling interests
1919	Ribble Motor Services set up
	Devon General set up, to NEC in 1922
1920	South Wales Commercial Motors (later Western Welsh) set up
	BAT buys shares in Ribble
1923	North Western formed by Tilling and BAT
1926	East Yorkshire formed by BAT
1927	East Midland Motor Services created from W. T. Underwood Ltd

1928	Barnsley & District renamed Yorkshire Traction
	BET and Tilling form Tilling & British Automobile Traction Ltd
1929	Western Welsh Omnibus company formed from South Wales Commercial Motors
	Northern General buys Wakefield's Motors
1929/30	Main-line railway companies buy into many BET and T&BAT companies
1931	BET buys National Electric Construction and bus companies Devon General, Mexborough & Swinton, City of Oxford, Rhondda and Western Welsh
	Sunderland District Omnibus to Northern General
1932	Devon General buys Grey Cars
	BET buys share in Hebble
1934	Rhondda Tramways Company renamed Rhondda Transport Company
1935	BMMO buys Stratford Blue
	Sheffield United Tours formed
1936	Northern General buys Tyneside tramways company
1942	T&BAT companies split between BET and Tilling groups
1951	BET forms Thomas Bros
	Last BET street trams run in Gateshead
1953	Greenslade's Tours bought by BET Group
1960	Swansea & Mumbles Railway closed
1961	Ribble buys Scout Motor Services
	Last Mexborough & Swinton trolleybus (last BET electric traction)
1962	South Wales Transport buys James, Ammanford
1965	Tyneside Tramways & Tramroads company renamed Tyneside Omnibus company
1967	BET sells UK bus interests to Transport Holding Company

ABOVE: Although City of Oxford Motor Services started out in 1906 as City of Oxford Electric Tramways Ltd, it never operated trams but replaced horsebuses with motorbuses from 1913. City of Oxford was one of BET's AEC fleets, and this 1970 AEC line-up at Gloucester Green in Oxford shows, from the left, a short-length (27ft 6in) AEC/Park Royal Bridgemaster 2B3RA 65-seater of 1962, a 1964 Reliance 2MU4RA with a Willowbrook 44-seat body, a 1958 Regent V LD3RA/Park Royal 65-seater, and a 1960 Regent V MD3RV/East Lancs lowbridge 58-seater. All wear the ornate maroon/red/duck-egg green livery that characterised the company's buses for many years. *Royston Morgan*

BELOW: The Devon General bus company was first set up in 1919 but found itself in competition with the National Electric Construction company's Torquay Tramways company, which had also introduced buses. The tramway company bought Devon General in 1922, and abandoned trams in 1934, by which time NEC had been bought by BET. In Torquay in 1969 is a 1966 Leyland Atlantean PDR1/1 with Willowbrook 75-seat body, bedecked with local advertising. *Royston Morgan*

ABOVE: When it was a Tilling & British Automobile Traction company, it seemed that North Western might have ended up in the Tilling camp following the 1942 division of the T&BAT company between BET and Tilling, but it passed to BET, even though its vehicle-buying policies continued to reflect Tilling policies for some years. This is a 1958 Leyland Tiger Cub PSUC1/2 with a dual-purpose Willowbrook body. *Dale Tringham*

BELOW: The East Midland company had its roots in the W. T. Underwood business, set up in 1920, and the East Midland name was adopted in 1927. Following railway investment, BET bought a 51% share. In 1973 a 1963 East Midland Leyland Leopard PDSU3/1R with 53-seat Willowbrook body leaves Doncaster. *Stewart J. Brown*

ABOVE: BET's companies in the North East, Yorkshire, the Midlands and South Wales tended to operate intensive services in heavily industrialised areas. This is a 1957 Hebble AEC Regent V D3RV with a Weymann 61-seat body, in Bradford in 1970. The tiny destination display contrasts with some of the more generous and informative layouts adopted by other BET companies. *H. J. Black*

BELOW: BET's companies in the south served more mixed areas, often with significant rural operations as well as seasonal services and a greater involvement in express services and general coaching. A 1968 Southdown Leyland Leopard PSU3/3RT with a Plaxton Panorama 49-seat body looks for day tour business in the traditional way at Brighton in 1972. *Stewart J. Brown*

The BET Bus Fleet | 2

The BET Group had a much less rigid approach to vehicle-buying than the state-owned Tilling Group. Tilling had, in effect, its own in-house manufacturers in Bristol and Eastern Coach Works (ECW). Both had started as parts of bus-operating companies and, particularly during the 1930s, had grown to supply a significant proportion of the buses bought by the companies that were particularly associated with Tilling. The redistribution of the Tilling and BET bus interests in 1942 had resulted in some companies 'changing sides', but when Tilling passed into state ownership in 1948, so did the Bristol chassis works and the ECW bodybuilding business. This meant that Bristol and ECW products were restricted to the state-owned fleets – in essence the Tilling and Scottish groups and London Transport (LT). While the Scottish Bus Group took a quota of Bristol and ECW products alongside proprietary models, and London Transport specified ECW bodies for its little Guy Vixen GS types, as well as for a prototype Routemaster, Tilling companies were by far the major customers; at the same time Bristol and ECW moved on from offering a range of rugged and conventional buses to developing innovative models tailored to meet the needs of its well-defined customer base.

There were also fans of Bristol chassis among the BET companies – notably North Western, whose 1960 fleet included rebodied prewar Bristol K and postwar Bristol L types, and Maidstone & District, nearly half of whose 1960 double-deck fleet was on Bristol chassis.

The nearest BET came to having an in-house supplier was the Birmingham & Midland Motor Omnibus Co (BMMO), which in prewar days had supplied chassis to other associated companies, but in the postwar period was building only for Midland Red.

The BET fleets were important customers for the UK's bus builders. They bought around 850 buses each year and while this buying power meant that BET could negotiate some very keen prices, the prospect of volume business – and, most importantly, continuing volume business – was essential for the builders who wanted to keep their production lines busy and guarantee employment for their workforce.

The arrival of chassis builders like Scania and Volvo into the UK market only happened in the 1970s, so during the 1960s BET – like virtually every UK customer – only bought chassis and bodies built in the UK. The only exceptions at this time were a handful of coach operators that had been attracted by early imports of coach bodies by Salvador Caetano (Portugal) and Van Hool (Belgium), while Mercedes-Benz tried several times to break into the UK market with complete coaches and, like the others, eventually succeeded. But the move to imported buses and coaches really took off in the 1970s, by which time BET's UK bus operations had passed to NBC. And even then NBC would pursue a very definite buy-British policy.

There were nominally 16 UK-based chassis-builders offering models aimed at home market customers during

RIGHT: Among the oldest-looking buses still running in BET fleets well into the 1960s were Dennis Lancet J10s with Strachan 38-seat rear-entrance bodies, dating from 1950. The conductress leafs through her newspaper while the bus sits in Guildford in 1961.
Martin Llewellyn/Omnicolour

the 1960s, though in reality the market was dominated by a small group of important players.

BET's 1960 fleet was dominated by AECs and Leylands, perhaps inevitably as these were Britain's two major chassis suppliers. But that didn't mean that other makes were frozen out, and although BET had its favoured suppliers it was prepared to allow its operating companies to buy less conventional types, and often these gave BET first-hand experience of types that found their way into other fleets.

AEC and Leyland had emerged during the late 1920s as the UK's two principal chassis builders, certainly in terms of their production output and their ability to handle the substantial orders that were placed as buses became more sophisticated and cost-effective and many fleets moved to replace their ageing tramway systems or upgrade their motorbus fleets. Both companies also produced trucks, and designed and produced their own engines, gearboxes and most major components, which gave them great flexibility and their development costs could be shared between their bus and truck ranges.

AEC – the Associated Equipment Co – had its roots in the vehicle-building works of the London General Omnibus Co and hit the ground running in 1912 producing substantial orders for LGOC. The creation of AEC was to allow it to compete for business in the open market and BET companies were among its early customers outside London. Its fortunes improved after the introduction of the Regal single-deck and Regent double-deck chassis in 1929, models that would gradually be developed and improved over the next 20 to 40 years.

During this period the Regal and Regent were offered increasingly with diesel rather than petrol engines, and there were the options of preselective and later automatic gearboxes, and air rather than vacuum brakes, as bus chassis grew longer in line with changing legislation. Two-axle single-deckers that could be no more than 27ft 6ins long in 1945 could be up to 30ft long from 1950, and this was still the maximum length in 1960. Two-axle double-deckers in 1945 were 26ft long in 1945, 27ft long from 1950 and in 1956 this was increased to 30ft, which was the situation in 1960.

Engines were firmly at the front on the great majority of buses and coaches until the 1950s, with drivers sitting alongside the engine – the classic half-cab arrangement. There had been attempts to produce chassis with engines at the side, under the floor and at the rear, and AEC had built the side-engined Q chassis in the 1930s and had developed an underfloor-engined model that was stillborn with the outbreak of the Second World War. This appeared a decade later as the Regal IV, and BET companies were early customers, for while the position of the engine meant that these buses were higher-built, the absence of any engine intrusion in the passenger saloon meant that up to 45 seats could be fitted in 30ft-long form, a significant increase on the 35/38-seaters that were the norm up to 1950. High-capacity buses were important for many BET Group fleets, but so was economical operation and the heavyweight Regal IV was no longer the first choice when AEC introduced the lighter-weight and more fuel-efficient Reliance, which quickly became a BET favourite.

Double-deck development had been less dramatic, although AEC did dabble with an underfloor-engined double-decker, which was sampled by several of the major fleets but found to be impractical. The typical BET double-decker of the early 1950s was a front-engined half-cab model with a body seating 56-62 passengers in normal-height 'highbridge' layout with central gangways on each deck, or 53-59 passengers in the 'lowbridge' layout, with a sunken side gangway to the upper deck and bench seating, to bring the bus within the target height of no more than around 13ft 6in – highbridge buses were typically up to 1ft higher. Outside the operations in the UK's main cities, which could normally use highbridge buses, the proliferation of low railway bridges meant that lowbridge buses – and often high-capacity single-deckers if the bridge was even lower – had to be used; in some cases the height of double-deckers was dictated by the clearance in bus garages. When 30ft-long double-deckers were legalised the seating capacities could be increased to 72/74 in highbridge form and 67 in lowbridge form.

The main external change to double-deckers in the 1950s was the widespread adoption of 'new-look' front ends, where the radiator was enclosed behind a metal cover, a fashion that had been started by Midland Red on its own-make double-deckers and then by Foden on its postwar front-engined models, and by operators like Birmingham City Transport. A new-look front was intended to give buses a more contemporary appearance, but many operators, including some significant BET fleets, continued to specify exposed radiators; one argument was that mechanical components were more easily accessible with an exposed radiator.

AEC's double-deck range received a new-look front in the 1950s, the most familiar being the design on the Regent V, with a stylised AEC radiator, complete with the AEC triangle badge. The Regent V also heralded a move to lighter-weight construction, and with pressure on bodybuilders to design lightweight bodies, the unladen weight of double-deckers dropped during the 1950s, permitting higher seating capacities.

Bristol and ECW products, still restricted to state-owned fleets, had shown the way with the Lodekka model, first introduced in 1949 and using ingenious chassis design to produce a double-decker that provided normal seating on both decks within the 13ft 6in height limit. Some BET companies may well have cast envious eyes on the local Tilling fleets with their Lodekkas, and AEC saw a market for a similarly flexible double-decker, producing the Bridgemaster in 1956 with more than half an eye on BET business. This incorporated some of the advanced features of the Routemaster, which AEC was building for London Transport at the time, but the Bridgemaster was not a great success; BET fleets took delivery of nearly two-thirds of the 179 Bridgemasters built.

The Bridgemaster had been designed as an integral bus with Park Royal bodywork, and AEC went on to develop another lowheight double-decker, this time a chassis, the Renown, that could be fitted with any bodywork. Again, BET fleets were the best customers, taking more than 60% of the 251 built. And it was largely the same BET companies that bought both models – City of Oxford, East Yorkshire, South Wales and Western Welsh.

AEC is probably best remembered for the Routemaster bus, developed with London Transport and regarded as one of the most iconic double-deckers of all time, and although it was undoubtedly a sophisticated and attractive model, it remained largely a bus used for London work except for the 50 Leyland-engined forward entrance examples bought by Northern General in 1964/65 for interurban services in north-east England.

AEC's conventional double-deck model was still popular with some BET fleets into the 1960s, and late-model

RIGHT: Operators that would have preferred to continue buying their favoured standard types in the early post-war years sometimes had to take other types if they were to replace older buses. Midland Red, which had built the great majority of its buses for more than 20 years, bought 100 of these AEC Regents with bodywork by Brush and Metro-Cammell in 1946. This is a Metro-Cammell-bodied example at Leicester in 1961; the bodywork is very much to Midland Red specification, with full-width front end.
Peter G. Smith/Omnicolour

Regent Vs went to Devon General and South Wales, both long-time AEC customers. In spite of competition from Leyland's Leopard, the AEC Reliance sold steadily into some BET fleets right to the end of BET influence: Aldershot & District, Devon General, East Kent, East Midland and South Wales took late deliveries, as did some of the coaching fleets – the Reliance was well regarded for coaching duties – like Hebble, Neath & Cardiff and Sheffield United.

Bristol had again led the way with a practical rear-engined single-decker, the RE model that was at the time restricted to state-owned companies, so AEC rushed to produce an equivalent, the Swift, which never enjoyed the reputation of AEC's earlier models. It was bought by City of Oxford, East Kent and East Midland.

AEC's influence waned during the 1960s following the first phase in a series of acquisitions and mergers that would change the face of the UK vehicle-manufacturing industry. AEC had broadened its portfolio in 1948 when it bought two smaller chassis-builders, Crossley and Maudslay, to form Associated Commercial Vehicles. The following year ACV bought two prominent coachbuilders, Park Royal and Roe.

But its arch-rival, Leyland was also on the acquisition trail. In 1951 it had bought Albion, and in 1962 acquired AEC and its associates. By the end of the 1960s Leyland would control most of its rival bus builders, and the inevitable outcome was rationalisation and the removal of overlapping models. During the 1960s AEC was allowed to develop its own models, notably the Swift, but the Reliance, Renown and Regent V would be the last of the distinguished line of true AECs.

Leyland was the other major supplier to BET fleets, and, like AEC, had been involved with the group from the early days. Leyland Motors had grown from its days building steam vehicles at Leyland, Lancashire at the end of the 19th century to become a major truck and bus manufacturer. Like AEC, its fortunes really changed later in the 1920s when it developed its six-cylinder Tiger single-deck and Titan double-deck models, in 1927, and quickly recognised the potential advantages of the diesel engine in the 1930s. Leyland was unusual among UK bus chassis builders in that it also built bodywork for its own chassis, and many operators bought complete vehicles from Leyland. The original Leyland Titan TD1 model of 1927 introduced the concept of lowbridge double-deckers within an amazing overall height of 12ft 10in, considerably less than its contemporaries. Leyland worked with London Transport on underfloor- and rear-engined single-deckers in the 1930s and was experimenting with rear-engined models of its own.

After the Second World War Leyland continued with updated versions of its Tiger and Titan ranges, but also recognised that the underfloor-engined layout was the way ahead for single-deckers. It developed the integrally-constructed Olympic with Metro-Cammell, but majored on separate chassis, the heavyweight Royal Tiger and the lightweight Tiger Cub. BET fleets took deliveries of all of these models.

Leyland advanced the design of double-deckers with its rear-engined Atlantean model in 1956, and again BET fleets were target customers, taking many of the early examples after the Atlantean went into production in 1958/59. Some operators embraced the Atlantean from the start, persevering with it in spite of teething problems that became apparent in the early days. Others tried Atlanteans and quickly went back to conventional front-engined double-deckers, while some resolutely stuck with front-engined models as long as they could, only relenting when the government's New Bus Grant scheme signalled the end of traditional front-engined buses.

Leyland's other major success with BET fleets was the Leopard, which in 36ft length with bodywork typically seating 53 passengers, offered a more flexible alternative to the unpopular lowbridge double-decker. Leyland also developed rear-engined single-deckers – the Panther and the lighter-weight Panther Cub – and while these were chosen by several BET fleets, they often proved to be less reliable than the sturdy and straightforward Leopard.

Leyland's ambitions to be the UK's major truck and bus builder started with the significant 'merger' with AEC in 1962, and gained momentum with the share exchange in 1965 with state-owned Bristol and Eastern Coach Works, which brought Bristol chassis and ECW bodies back on to the open market for the first time since 1948, and BET fleets – some of them faithful customers in previous times – took advantage of their ability to buy Bristol models again, and particularly the RE single-deck range.

Other changes in ownership had brought Daimler and Guy under Jaguar ownership, and in 1966 Jaguar merged with British Motor Corporation to form British Motor Holdings (BMH), a significant force in the car market. Leyland had mopped up car-makers Rover and Standard-Triumph and it seemed to make sense in 1968 to merge Leyland and BMH to create a giant entity, British Leyland Motor Corporation. Time has shown that this was an unwieldy giant and that the bus division suffered while millions of pounds were pumped into the ailing car division.

The main consequences of the birth of British Leyland would become evident in the 1970s, after BET had sold out to the Transport Holding Company, but BL made a start by cutting out duplication in its acquired models and paving the way to a situation where bus operators had considerably less choice.

Guy Motors was another long-standing vehicle manufacturer, but it really came to the fore during the Second World War when it was decided that the company would be one of a small number permitted to build double-

RIGHT: Midland Red had received utility Guy Arabs during the Second World War, and in 1949 went on to buy 20 of these Guy Arab IIIs with Guy 56-seat bodies, as seen at Dudley in 1962. *Chris Aston/ Omnicolour*

deck bus chassis for essential customers. The utility Guy Arab found its way into fleets throughout the UK and its rugged reliability appealed to many operators, who continued to buy successive Arab models into the 1950s. Several BET fleets stuck with Guy models for some years – notably East Kent and Maidstone & District in the south-east, and Northern General, which also bought Guy single-deckers. Unfortunately Guy's attempt to break into the lucrative double-deck market of the late 1950s cut no ice with BET fleets; the nearest the advanced front-engined Wulfrunian model got to BET sales was with deliveries to County Motors, the firm jointly owned by BET's Yorkshire Traction and Yorkshire Woollen companies, and independent West Riding, where West Riding – by far the largest customer for the Wulfrunian – influenced County's double-deck orders.

Daimler, on the other hand, was a bit of a slow burner. Like Guy, its chassis output was limited, compared with market leaders AEC and Leyland, and Daimler had established its niche as a firm favourite with municipal fleets, who found that the combination of economical Gardner engines and preselective gearboxes were ideal for intense urban work. Before the Second World War, Trent had been a faithful Daimler customer and in the postwar years Potteries had bought Daimler models, but Daimler's fortunes changed when it developed its answer to the Leyland Atlantean, the rear-engined Fleetline double-deck model that introduced Daimlers to a new audience. Indeed, some of the new customers had been early customers for the Leyland Atlantean and had previously been staunchly Leyland fleets.

Trent and Potteries embraced the Fleetline, but among the more unexpected converts were City of Oxford, Midland Red, Southdown, Yorkshire Traction and Yorkshire Woollen.

Daimler blotted its copybook with the rear-engined single-deck Roadliner model, a promising chassis that was fatally damaged by the choice of an unfamiliar and unreliable Cummins engine. One BET company, Potteries, was the major customer for this flawed model and rapidly disposed of its Roadliner fleet. Daimler restored its reputation with a single-deck version of the successful Fleetline, and this was bought by Gateshead & District, Maidstone & District, Northern General, City of Oxford, Potteries, Sunderland District, Tynemouth & District and Yorkshire Traction. BET companies accounted for nearly one in 10 of all Fleetline sales.

In many ways the most interesting vehicle policy in the BET Group was that pursued by Midland Red. This was by far the largest BET fleet, averaging 1,800 buses for most of the 1960s, and half as big again as the second largest BET fleet, Ribble. Although most of the big central workshops that served BET companies could turn their hand to major chassis and body work, including major conversions that stopped just short of being completely new vehicles, Midland Red designed and built its own vehicles from the ground up. While the Tilling Group had Bristol and Eastern Coach Works supplying all but a handful of their annual vehicle requirements, Midland Red's BMMO types were built purely for its own use – and even then it had to augment these with proprietary buses and coaches. Before the Second World War Midland Red had built chassis for other operators, but as its own fleet grew it required to retain all of its production capacity.

BMMO vehicles were not clones of the vehicles other BET fleets were buying. They were unusual – some might say quirky – but they were designed very much with Midland

ABOVE: Southdown, with a strong Leyland tradition, had received Guy Arabs during the war and continued to buy Guys into the mid-1950s; in Brighton in 1968 is one of 48 Arab IVs with elegant Park Royal 59-seat bodies delivered in 1955/56. *Mark Page*

Red's operating conditions in mind. BMMO led the way with volume production of underfloor-engined single-deckers immediately after the war, and experimented with a number of advanced features, many of which found their way into production batches, sometimes long before the mainstream manufacturers followed suit.

When it needed more vehicles than it could build in-house, Midland Red turned to other builders – buying AEC Regent and Guy Arab double-deckers in the 1940s, Leyland Titan double-deckers in the 1950s, and Daimler Fleetline double-deckers and Leyland Leopard single-deckers in the 1960s. But these were easily outnumbered by BMMO-built S type single-deckers, D type double-deckers and C type coaches. The very last BMMO types were S23 buses built in 1970, after BET had become part of the National Bus Company.

Although BET had its favoured suppliers – and negotiated favourable deals with these manufacturers who were rewarded with repeated volume business – there was still room for other firms to win BET orders.

Dennis, a major player in the UK bus scene since the 1990s, was well down the pecking-order in the 1950s and 1960s, but it did have a few faithful followers among the BET fleets. Aldershot & District, serving the Dennis hometown of Guildford, was an obvious customer and its 1960 fleet included front-engined Lancet single-deckers, Falcon normal control single-deckers, Lance double-deckers and Loline lowheight double-deckers; the Loline started as a Bristol Lodekka built under licence, and more Lolines would be bought during the 1960s, by Aldershot & District, which became the largest customer for this type, but also City of

Oxford and North Western, both fleets looking for low-height double-deckers. East Kent favoured Dennis single-deckers in the 1940s and early 1950s, buying normal control Falcons and front-engined and underfloor-engined Lancets.

Albion, part of Leyland since 1951, became more associated with models it developed for the Scottish Bus Group, but several BET fleets bought Albions. The little underfloor-engined Nimbus, a midibus before its time, was bought by Devon General, Maidstone & District and Western Welsh for more marginal services where a short-length 30-seater was adequate. The Aberdonian, a lighter-weight version of Leyland's Tiger Cub, was bought by East Yorkshire, Northern General, North Western and Potteries. The Lowlander, essentially Leyland's answer to low-height double-deck models like the AEC Bridgemaster and Renown and the Dennis Loline, was chosen by East Midland and Ribble.

Atkinson, the truck builder based near Preston, was persuaded to develop single-deck bus chassis for customers looking for the combination of a Gardner engine and conventional transmission – a combination that Bristol catered for before it passed into state control. North Western, a firm Bristol fan, bought 16 of Atkinson's Alpha model in 1951/52. Atkinson then disappeared from BET's list of preferred suppliers and North Western mainly turned to AEC Reliances and Leyland Tiger Cubs.

Beadle blossomed in the years following the Second World War, as a bodybuilder, as a builder of integral buses using existing parts, and developed its own range of integral buses and coaches. As a Kent-based bodybuilder its products could be found in the East Kent, Maidstone & District and Southdown fleets. Its semi-integral full-size single-deckers, using parts from prewar AECs and Leylands, were found in the same three south-eastern fleets, as well as in the East Yorkshire, Yorkshire Traction and Yorkshire Woollen fleets; these proved useful low-cost crowd-movers in the 1950s but were being phased out of BET fleets by the early 1960s.

Beadle's own integral models, using Commer TS3 two-stroke engines, were found as coaches in the Devon General, East Kent, Southdown, and Yorkshire Woollen fleets, and as buses with Devon General, Northern General, Potteries and Yorkshire Traction.

Another bodybuilder producing integrals in addition to building bodies on mainstream chassis was Harrington of Hove, which developed the integral Contender, using the Commer TS3 engine, and Maidstone & District bought 11 of these as buses and three as coaches in 1955.

Commer vied with Bedford to supply full-size lighter-weight coach chassis in the 1950s and its Avenger was bought with coach bodywork by Maidstone & District (with petrol engine) and Southdown (with TS3 diesel engine).

Bedford was by far the most popular supplier of front-engined lightweight coach chassis, and many BET fleets augmented their heavier-weight coaches with small batches of Bedfords, usually SB types for private hire work, though North Western did buy a batch of 10 three-axle VAL models with low-built Strachans bus bodywork for a route that passed under the 8ft 9in canal bridge at Dunham Massey.

Ford used the Thames name for its first foray into building bus/coach chassis, and the Thames Trader quickly established itself as the main rival to Bedford's SB. Again, most Thames models for BET fleets were bought in small quantities for local tour and private hire work. Under the Ford name, its models would prove popular with former BET fleets after the sale to Transport Holding Company, and in NBC's later days, Ford Transit minibuses could be found in many fleets.

Of some 11,700 buses and coaches in the BET fleets in 1960, just over 43% were Leylands (more than 5,000), with AECs (2,600) and Guys (1,000-plus) in second and fourth place. In third place, with more than 1,600 vehicles, was BMMO, all in the Midland Red fleet. And it was a long way down to the next most popular make – Dennis, at more than 400. The pecking order would change during the 1960s, with Leyland, AEC and BMMO in the top three places, and Daimler coming up fast with nearly 700 buses.

There were dedicated AEC fleets, which rarely bought anything else. City of Oxford, Devon General, Hebble, South Wales and Yorkshire Woollen were confirmed AEC single-deck and double-deck customers, while Rhondda bought AEC double-deckers but Leyland single-deckers, and there were many more fleets that bought only AEC single-deckers, often alongside Leyland double-deckers. There were many more committed Leyland customers, especially as the 1960s continued, and many fleets turned to the rear-engined Atlantean double-decker (AEC had no equivalent model) and the underfloor-engined Leopard single-decker. Even the staunchly pro-AEC Devon General turned to Atlanteans in the early 1960s – before returning to AEC Regents.

For fleets requiring lowheight double-deckers there were various choices, as we have seen. Some continued to buy conventional double-deckers with side-gangway lowbridge bodies – the last were AEC Regent V/East Lancs supplied to

LEFT: Maidstone & District also operated Guys in the post-war years. This 1954 Arab IV with a 58-seat Weymann body was transferred from its associated Chatham & District fleet in 1955. In the background are Maidstone Corporation Leyland Titans.
Martin Llewellyn/Omnicolour

City of Oxford in 1960. Others tried Leyland's fairly unsatisfactory semi-lowheight Atlantean model. And a few turned to the breed of front-engined lowheight double-deck models that appeared in the 1950s and 1960s, following the success of the Bristol/ECW Lodekka, which was restricted to state-owned fleets. As we have seen, integrally constructed AEC/Park Royal Bridgemasters joined the City of Oxford, East Kent, East Yorkshire, South Wales and Western Welsh fleets. The successor to the Bridgemaster, the AEC Renown, went to the same fleets. The Dennis Loline went to Aldershot & District, City of Oxford and North Western, and the Leyland-Albion Lowlander to East Midland, Ribble and Yorkshire Woollen.

But increasingly it was the Leyland Atlantean that came to dominate double-deck deliveries to BET fleets, even though a few operators held out against its appeal and turned to lowheight models, or continued to buy big front-engined double-deckers as long as they could – East Kent and Southdown were notable examples.

And some turned to Daimler's new rear-engined Fleetline when it appeared in the early 1960s. Maidstone & District, Potteries and Trent – all fleets that had bought early Atlanteans – moved on to the Fleetline for their double-deck requirements, as did Hebble, Tynemouth and Yorkshire Woollen and, perhaps the most surprising of all, Midland Red. Most of Midland Red's double-deck requirements for many years had been met by its own-make BMMO types, but from 1963 it took batches of Fleetlines, ending up with more than 300 of them.

BET fleets had quickly embraced the underfloor-engined single-decker when it appeared on the market in the early 1950s, firstly with heavyweight models like AEC's Regal IV and Leyland's Olympian and Royal Tiger, then with the lighter-weight models that largely replaced them on the home market, the AEC Reliance and Leyland Tiger Cub. When longer buses were legalised in 1961 many BET companies turned to the 36-foot-long version of the Reliance and Leyland's new Leopard chassis. With seats typically for 53 passengers, these new single-deckers were seen by some companies as an alternative to double-deckers, particularly the outmoded lowbridge types that often only had seats for 55 passengers.

Reliances and Leopards were also popular for coaching work, and several fleets also turned to lightweight coaches for day-tour and private-hire work, taking small batches of Bedford and Thames models. Commer coaches were the alternative to Bedfords in some fleets, and several BET fleets had small numbers of them, though Southdown amassed 45 between 1959 and 1962 with Burlingham and Harrington coach bodies.

There were also the Beadle-Commer integral coaches in the Southdown and Yorkshire Woollen fleets, and Beadle-Commer integral buses had been supplied to Devon General, Northern General, Potteries and Yorkshire Traction. Maidstone & District had received Harrington-Commer integral buses and coaches in the 1950s.

Smaller buses rarely figured in BET fleets, in spite of the many rural routes that were operated, though the midi-size Albion Nimbus was favoured by Devon General, Maidstone & District and Western Welsh in the early 1960s, and Aldershot & District and East Kent took the normal control Dennis Falcon.

BET fleets were slightly more wary of the new breed of rear-engined single-deck models that appeared from the mid-1960s, but some fleets sampled the new types. AEC's Swift was supplied to East Kent, East Midland and City of Oxford, and Leyland's Panther to East Yorkshire, Northern General and Ribble. The lighter-weight Panther Cub went to East Yorkshire and Thomas Bros. Potteries chose the Daimler Roadliner, and several fleets – East Midland, North Western, Ribble, Southdown and Trent – opted for the Bristol RELL. Other former BET companies would continue with the Bristol RE into the early 1970s, while others turned to Daimler's single-deck Fleetline.

For their bus and coach bodies, BET fleets had to turn to a group of major bodybuilders with the capacity to supply BET as well as the municipal and large independent fleets. So in the 1950s single-deck bus bodies typically came from Metro-Cammell, Weymann and Willowbrook, to be joined in increasing numbers in the 1960s by Alexander and Marshall bodies. Single-deck coach bodies were largely from Duple, Harrington and Plaxton. Double-deck bodies were supplied by Metro-Cammell, Northern Counties, Park Royal, Roe, Weymann and Willowbrook, with smaller quantities from East Lancs but increasing deliveries from Alexander during the 1960s.

Some operators formed close working relationships with bodybuilders and, where possible, stuck with that builder's products.

Certain chassis tended to be associated with particular bodybuilders, like Alexander bodies on Albion Lowlanders, and Park Royal bodies on AEC Renowns, and although BET fleets took these combinations, they also turned to other builders on these chassis. The early Leyland Atlanteans tended to be bodied by Metro-Cammell in normal-height form and Weymann in semi-lowbridge form, but Roe also

bodied early Atlanteans and from the mid-1960s Alexander and to a lesser degree Northern Counties and Willowbrook built on Atlantean. While Alexander became a mainstream BET supplier, Northern Counties and Willowbrook lacked the capacity to supply bodies in large numbers. Northern Counties famously bodied the 'Queen Mary' Leyland Titan PD3s for Southdown as well as single-deckers, and Yorkshire Traction and the Welsh fleets were other good Northern Counties customers.

Park Royal could also supply the quantities BET required, and as well as types like the AEC Bridgemaster and Routemaster that could only be supplied with Park Royal bodies, there were regulars like East Kent (on AEC Reliance and Regent V and Daimler Fleetline), East Yorkshire (on Fleetline and AEC Renown), City of Oxford (on AEC Reliance and Renown), and South Wales (on Reliance, Regent V and Renown). As parts of the same group, the AEC/Park Royal combination was an obvious one, but Park Royal also bodied smaller quantities of Leyland single-deckers. Park Royal's associate, Roe, was heavily involved in building bodies for municipal operators, but could also share the load when Park Royal was particularly busy with big batches like the London Routemasters. As well as early Atlanteans, Roe supplied bodies to BET's Yorkshire fleets.

Willowbrook relied heavily on BET Group business, supplying standard bus bodies on AEC Reliance and Leyland Tiger Cub and Leopard chassis right through the 1960s, alongside Marshall, which emerged as a major bodybuilder in the 1960s and supplied large numbers of standard BET bus bodies on Reliance, Tiger Cub and Leopard chassis. Alexander broadened its customer base in the 1960s, first with standard BET-style single-deck bodies, and then with its

LEFT: Some BET companies opted to have older Leyland Tiger single-deckers rebuilt and rebodied as double-deckers; this is one of nine PS2 chassis delivered in the early post-war years with neighbouring Yorkshire Woollen and fitted in 1963 with 63-seat Northern Counties forward-entrance bodies for Yorkshire Traction, here in snowy Huddersfield in 1963 passing a Leyland Comet flatbed lorry.
Martin Llewellyn/Omnicolour

LEFT: Although Aldershot & District was the main Dennis customer in the BET Group, East Kent also favoured the type, for its single-deck purchases. This is one of 30 Dennis Lancet LU2s with Duple 41-seat centre-entrance coach bodies, heading through Park Gate for London in 1962. *Martin Llewellyn/Omnicolour*

RIGHT: BET fleets tended to buy full-size buses and coaches, with occasional batches of smaller-capacity buses for rural routes. Maidstone & District and Western Welsh chose Albion's midi-size Nimbus; this NS3N was one of 15 bought by Maidstone & District in 1960 fitted with Harrington 30-seat bodies. Note the trim on both wheels and the characteristic M&D cream panel below the windscreens. *Dale Tringham*

own body styles on a range of single-deck and double-deck chassis. Other smaller builders picked up some BET bus business, like East Lancs on AEC Regent V and Dennis Loline, and Harrington on AEC Reliance, but Harrington became an important supplier of single-deck coach bodies when it introduced its Cavalier body range, and it competed for this business with Duple and Plaxton.

Like bus operators in all of the sectors, BET fleets were involved in rebuilding and rebodying prewar and wartime buses in the early postwar years, and while the pace slowed down as new buses started to come through, some fleets continued the practice into the 1950s and 1960s, converting what were now unfashionable Leyland Tiger single-deckers to Titan PD2 standard and sending them to be rebodied as double-deckers. Yorkshire Woollen had Tiger PS1s rebodied by Metro-Cammell in the mid-1950s, and Yorkshire Traction had PS1s rebodied by Roe between

1955 and 1957. These buses had rear-entrance bodies, but in 1960–63 Yorkshire Traction had Tiger PS2s rebodied with forward-entrance bodies by Northern Counties and Roe; Stratford Blue also received a similar Roe rebody in 1961, and Yorkshire Woollen received six Roe rebodies in 1963.

Beadle used prewar AEC and Leyland chassis to produce semi-integral single-deck buses and coaches in the 1950s.

At the time BET sold out to the Transport Holding Co, its combined fleet was just 5% down on its 1960 total, at just over 11,000 vehicles. Leyland still dominated, but slightly down at just under 5,000, with AEC increasing to more than 3,400 and BMMO dropping to just over 1,300, reflecting the increasing use of Leyland single-deckers and Daimler double-deckers in the Midland Red fleet. The Dennis total dropped from more than 400 to just over 200, and Guy from 1,000-plus to just 200.

ABOVE: Alexander bodywork became more popular among BET fleets during the 1960s. North Western took both single-deck and double-deck Alexander bodies; this 1961 AEC Reliance 2MU3RA has a 41-seat dual-purpose Alexander body and represents an interesting marriage of BET and Scottish Bus Group design features. *Mark Page*

BELOW: BET companies were early customers for the Leyland Atlantean, including the awkward semi-lowheight version, represented by this 1959 PDR1/1 with a 73-seat Weymann body for Yorkshire Traction, in Huddersfield in 1972. *H. J. Black*

ABOVE: There was scope for BET companies to buy buses in small batches for their particular requirements. In 1959 and 1963 South Wales bought eight of these lowheight (8ft 11in) single-deckers based on AEC Regent V 2D3RA double-deck chassis with 37-seat Roe bodies. They were for a route in the Llanelly dock area that had restricted clearance. *Royston Morgan*

BELOW: The last of many AECs for Devon General were Reliances bought in 1971. This is a 6MU3R model with a Willowbrook 41-seat body that was new in that year. These were also the last new buses delivered in the traditional Devon General livery. *Royston Morgan*

ABOVE: Although Leyland did eventually produce a true lowheight Atlantean, Daimler's Fleetline was a lowheight chassis from the start and several BET fleets that had bought Atlanteans turned to Fleetlines. Trent was one of them, but had only a limited requirement for lowheight buses; this Fleetline CRG6LX with a normal-height Alexander body was new in 1968. Behind it is a Midland General Bristol VRT with an ECW body; control of this former Tilling company passed to Trent in 1972, under the National Bus Company. *Royston Morgan*

BELOW: The archetypal BET single-decker of the 1960s was the Leyland Leopard with this style of bodywork, built by several bodybuilders. This PSU3/2R with a Willowbrook 53-seat body, seen in Dewsbury in 1972, was new to Yorkshire Woollen in 1965. *H. J. Black*

ABOVE: City of Oxford was a staunch AEC fan and bought examples of AEC's Regent, Bridgemaster and Renown double-deck models. Here at Gloucester Green bus station in Oxford in 1969 are, on the left, one of the short-length AEC/Park Royal Renown 3B3RA 65-seater bought in 1963 and, in the background, a short-length 65-seat AEC/Park Royal Bridgemaster 2B3RA of 1962. *Ted Jones*

BELOW: The AEC Reliance was a popular choice for coaching work and this is a 1969 South Wales Reliance 8U3ZR with Duple Commander 44-seat body in Ludlow in 1971. *Ted Jones*

ABOVE: For most of its existence Ribble favoured locally-built Leyland buses, like this 1956 Titan PD2/13 with 61-seat Metro-Cammell Orion bodywork on a local service in Preston in 1969. *Ted Jones*

BELOW: The Leyland Tiger Cub with Weymann bodywork was a staple in many BET fleets in the 1950s and 1960s. This 1956 East Midland PSUC1/1 with 44-seat body is seen leaving Chesterfield bus station in 1970. *Ted Jones*

ABOVE: North Western bought the Dennis Loline and AEC Renown for its lowheight double-deck requirements before moving to the Daimler Fleetline with Alexander body, as here at Blackpool Coliseum coach station in 1965, where a 1965 CRG6 75-seater has recently arrived on the X60 service from Manchester. Behind, also on the X60, is another Fleetline, a Northern Counties-bodied example from the independent Lancashire United fleet. *Ted Jones*

BELOW: The distinctive lines of Midland Red's BMMO-built S17 class of 36-foot-long single-deck buses. These were built in the mid-1960s and this is a 1965 example with 52-seat BMMO bodywork completed by Willowbrook. It is seen at Shrewsbury in 1969. *Ted Jones*

ABOVE: Ribble bought 16 Albion Lowlander LR1 in 1964/65, with 72-seat Alexander bodies that incorporated a variation of the frontal styling applied to Ribble's Leyland Titan PD3s. A 1964 example is at Fleetwood Ferry in 1969. *Ted Jones*

BELOW: City of Oxford embellished the functional lines of the standard BET style body with its characteristic 'vee' on the front panels, as on this 1963 AEC Reliance 2MU3RV with 44-seat Marshall bodywork seen in High Street, Oxford in 1972. *Ted Jones*

ABOVE: The semi-lowheight version of the Leyland Atlantean PDR1/1 with Weymann bodywork was a less than satisfactory solution to building a rear-engined lowheight double-decker. Maidstone & District was an early customer for the Atlantean, and this is a 1959 73-seater in Bexhill in 1969. Maidstone & District, like some other BET fleets, turned to Daimler's Fleetline, as it offered a proper lowheight layout. *Ted Jones*

BELOW: The shape of the North Bar in Beverley dictated the contours of the upper deck of many of East Yorkshire's double-deckers. When the company bought lowheight AEC/Park Royal Renowns, some had tapered upper decks, like this 1965 70-seat 3B3RA model at Scarborough in 1971. *Ted Jones*

ABOVE: The advance in vehicle design is illustrated by these two Thomas Bros single-deckers in Port Talbot in 1965. In front is a 1963 AEC Reliance 4MU4RA with 53-seat Marshall body, and in the distance a 1954 Leyland Tiger Cub PSUC1/1 with Saro 44-seat body. *Ted Jones*

BELOW: Even staunch Leyland fans like Ribble succumbed to the charms of the Bristol RELL model, and although its first batch had Leyland engines, this 1969 example, seen in Cleveleys when new, is an RELL6G with Gardner engine. It has 41-seat two-door ECW bodywork. *Ted Jones*

THE BET BUS FLEET
IN 1959 AND 1968

	1959	1968
Aldershot & District	340 (203 s/d, 137 d/d)	285 (144 s/d, 141 d/d)
Blue Cars	32 (32 s/d)	
City of Oxford	245 (51 s/d, 194 d/d)	218 (91 s/d, 127 d/d
Devon General	312 (111 s/d, 201 d/d)	276 (137 s/d, 139 d/d)
East Kent	631(347 s/d, 284 d/d)	606 (336 s/d, 270 d/d)
East Midland	253 (157 s/d, 96 d/d)	224 (146 s/d, 78 d/d)
East Yorkshire	264 (93 s/d, 171 d/d)	253 (101 s/d, 152 d/d)
Gateshead & District	75 (75 d/d)	68 (68 d/d)
Greenslades	81 (81 s/d)	80 (80 s/d)
Hebble	94 (68 s/d, 26 d/d)	72 (53 s/d, 19 d/d)
James, Ammanford	36 (12 s/d, 24 d/d)	
Maidstone & District	842 (397 s/d, 445 d/d***)	753 (449 s/d, 304 d/d)
Mexborough & Swinton	46 (46 s/d***)	44 (19 s/d, 25 d/d)
Midland Red	1,839 (1,008 s/d, 831 d/d)	1,775 (936 s/d, 839 d/d)
Neath & Cardiff	33 (33 s/d)	32 (32 s/d)
North Western	586 (436 s/d, 150 d/d)	567 (379 s/d, 188 d/d)
Northern General	673 (456 s/d, 217 d/d)	593 (368 s/d, 225 d/d)
Potteries	503 (292 s/d, 211 d/d)	504 (297 s/d, 207 d/d)
Red Line	6 (6 s/d)	
Rhondda	197 (77 s/d, 120 d/d)	161 (65 s/d, 96 d/d)
Ribble	1,169 (525 s/d, 644 d/d)	1,093 (546 s/d, 547 d/d)
Sheffield United Tours	99 (99 s/d)	103 (103 s/d)
Southdown	987 (488 s/d, 499 d/d)	882 (530 s/d, 352 d/d)
South Wales	353 (110 s/d, 243 d/d***)	326 (99 s/d, 227 d/d)
Standerwick	104 (104 s/d)	82 (49 s/d, 33 d/d)
Stratford Blue	38 (18 s/d, 20 d/d)	44 (20 s/d, 24 d/d)
Sunderland District	103 (62 s/d, 41 d/d)	93 (56 s/d, 37 d/d)
Thomas Bros	48 (48 s/d)	52 (50 s/d, 2 d/d)
Trent	413 (213 s/d, 200 d/d)	377 (194 s/d, 183 d/d)
Tynemouth & District	82 (3 d/d, 79 d/d)	73 (4 s/d, 69 d/d)
Tyneside	18 (18 d/d)	16 (16 d/d)
Wakefield's	19 (14 s/d, 5 d/d)	15 (10 s/d, 5 d/d)
Western Welsh	695 (568 s/d, 127 d/d)	576 (397 s/d, 179 d/d)
Yorkshire Traction	371 (238 s/d, 133 d/d)	334 (203 s/d, 131 d/d)
Yorkshire Woollen	277 (130 s/d, 147 d/d)	242 (134 s/d, 108 d/d)
TOTALS	**11,864***	**10,819****

* The 1959 total of 11,864 comprised 6,542 single-deckers (55%) and 5,322 (45%) double-deckers

** The 1968 total of 10,819 comprised 6,028 (56%) single-deckers and 4,791 (44%) double-deckers.

*** The 1959 Maidstone & District double-deck total included 46 double-deck trolleybuses; the 1959 Mexborough & Swinton single-deck total included 30 trolleybuses; the 1959 South Wales double-deck total included 13 double-deck Swansea & Mumbles trams.

The size of the combined BET fleet dropped by 9% between 1959 and 1968, using figures from contemporary editions of The Little Red Book. This partly reflected cutbacks in more marginal services, but can also be explained by the increasing size of new buses. With many 36ft-long single-deck buses and coaches, and 30ft-long double-deckers including 78-seat Leyland Atlanteans, many fleets could offer the same number of seats for passengers with fewer buses, sometimes manifested in reduced frequencies. The five largest BET fleets over this period are shown in the table below.

1959			1968		
1	Midland Red	1,839	1	Midland Red	1,775
2	Ribble	1,169	2	Ribble	1,093
3	Southdown	987	3	Southdown	882
4	Maidstone & District	842	4	Maidstone & District	753
5	Western Welsh	695	5	East Kent	606

Although the total BET fleet size dropped by nearly 9% over the decade, the proportions of single-deckers and double-deckers remained very much the same, although there were significant changes in some individual fleets. Aldershot & District went from a single-deck:double-deck ratio of 60:40 in 1959 to 51:49 in 1968. City of Oxford went from 21:79 to 42:58, Devon General from 36:64 to 50:50, Maidstone & District from 47:53 to 60:40, Southdown from 49:51 to 60:40, and Western Welsh went the other way from 82:18 to 69:31. Other fleets that increased their double-deck fleets were Midland Red, North Western, Northern General and Yorkshire Traction.

BELOW: Midland Red retained its position as the largest BET Group fleet right through the 1960s. The proportion of its own-make BMMO buses remained high – more than four out of every five Midland Red buses was built by the company, like this 1963 example of the distinctive D9 type, seen at Burton on Trent. *Mark Page*

3 | BET in the North East

On a map the area served by BET's Northern General companies does looks small compared with that of its neighbouring Tilling company, United Automobile Services, yet this masks the fact that Northern operated in good bus territory and was one of BET's most profitable companies.

Its roots were in 19th-century tramways – Gateshead & District and Tynemouth & District – both of which were bought by BET in the closing years of that century and converted to electric traction. The Gateshead trams continued until 1951, and were widely regarded as the last BET-operated trams, although South Wales Transport did operate the Swansea & Mumbles railways for a brief period in 1959/60. The Tynemouth trams were replaced by buses in 1931.

Much earlier, in 1913, BET had formed the Northern General Transport Co Ltd to bring together the group's various transport interests, and started motorbus operations in 1914. Northern bought various other local companies, notably Sunderland District in 1931 and the Tyneside tramway company – which had abandoned trams in 1930 – in 1936. Although some of the acquisitions continued to

operate under their own names and in their own liveries, others like the Jarrow & District tramways acquired in 1929 did not; the Jarrow-South Shields tram route was replaced by Northern buses.

By 1960 the Northern companies had grown to a fleet of more than 900 buses. The 1962 fleet shows a drop to 883, with 611 in the main red Northern fleet, 95 in the blue Sunderland District fleet, 73 in the red Tynemouth fleet, 70 in the maroon Gateshead fleet, and 17 each in the green Tyneside and red Wakefield's fleets.

The Northern operating area stretched from Blyth and Tynemouth on the north bank of the River Tyne, west to Consett and south to Bishop Auckland, Middlesbrough,

BELOW: Northern General, taken with its subsidiary companies, was one of BET's largest fleets, and its bus-buying pattern did not always reflect that of other group companies. In 1960 there were more than 1,000 Guys in BET fleets, and Northern had the greatest concentration of these – more than 400. This is a Guy Arab IV with a Park Royal 63-seat body, one of 20 delivered in 1956. It is seen in Sunderland in 1966, preceded by a policeman and followed by a Rolls-Royce. *Chris Aston/Omnicolour*

Stockton and West Hartlepool, with the greatest concentration of services in the area bounded by South Shields, Sunderland, Durham, Chester le Street, Gateshead and Newcastle. Around and throughout Northern's territory was Tilling's giant United Auto company, with more than 1,000 buses operating in an area that stretched from Berwick through Northumberland and County Durham into Yorkshire. Some services were operated jointly by Northern and United.

There were other operators in Northern territory – municipal undertakings at Newcastle, South Shields and Sunderland (and on the fringes at Middlesbrough and Stockton) and some significant independent bus operators, notably OK of Bishop Auckland and Venture of Consett.

Northern had bought BMMO-built single-deckers in the late 1920s and went on to design and build its own advanced side-engined SE types in the 1930s. With many low railway bridges throughout its area, Northern had a high proportion of single-deck buses – nearly 60% of the 1962 fleet – and was always looking at ways to maximise seating capacity within the permitted legal dimensions.

The underfloor-engined single-decker allowed up to 44 or 45 seats within the 30-foot length permitted in the 1950s, and there were substantial numbers of AEC Reliances and Monocoaches, Guy Arab LUFs and Leyland Tiger Cubs in the 1962 fleet. There were also five of Leyland's lighter-weight Tiger Cub, the Albion Aberdonian, as well as the last of a large batch of front-engined Guy Arabs bought in 1949/50 with 38-seat Brush bodies. The choice of bodybuilder for the underfloor-engined single-deckers reflected BET's preferred suppliers at the time, so there were buses and dual-purpose vehicles by Alexander, Burlingham, Park Royal, Saunders-Roe, Weymann and Willowbrook, and the coaches had bodies by Harrington, Weymann and Willowbrook, as well as Picktree, a local builder. In 1962 Northern had received its first batch of Willowbrook-bodied 53-seat Leyland Leopard 36-footers, and these would become more common as the 1960s progressed.

Northern's double-deckers were all full-height buses, front-engined AECs, Guys and Leylands, and rear-engined Leylands. The AECs had Roe bodies; the Guys had Brush, Northern Coachbuilders, Park Royal or Weymann bodies; the front-engined Leylands had Leyland, Park Royal or Weymann bodies; and the rear-engined Leylands Roe or Weymann bodies. Northern was an early customer for Leyland's new Atlantean, buying its first in 1959, no doubt attracted by the seating capacity of 77 or 78.

BELOW: Northern operated an extensive touring programme, and in 1963 bought five of these Leyland Leopard PSU3/3Rs with Harrington Grenadier 44-seat coach bodies. One is seen heading through Leicester for the South West of England in 1968. *Dale Tringham*

ABOVE: Northern famously bought 50 AEC/Park Royal Routemasters in 1964/65, the only examples built for use outside London. This is one of the first 18, bought in 1964, with a 72-seat forward-entrance body. *Royston Morgan*

During the 1960s Northern dual-sourced its new buses and coaches from AEC and Leyland. AEC supplied Reliances – coaches bodied by Harrington and Plaxton, dual-purpose vehicles by Alexander and Weymann, and buses by Marshall and Willowbrook – and famously 50 forward-entrance Routemasters in 1964/65, the only ones built for operation outside London.

Leyland continued to supply Atlanteans right through to the end of the decade, with Alexander, Metro-Cammell or Roe bodies. Leyland's Leopard quickly became the chassis of choice for buses and dual-purpose vehicles, with bodies by Alexander, Marshall or Willowbrook. In 1969 Northern bought Marshall-bodied Leyland Panther buses, its first rear-engined single-deckers, and the first of a number bought by the group, acquired from other NBC companies. For Northern's extensive tour programme there were short-length Leopard/Harringtons and 36-foot Leopards with Harrington or Plaxton bodies. Unusual coaches were lightweight Bedford SB5s with Harrington bodies supplied in 1963.

Sunderland District's 1962 fleet was 55% single-deck, with two AEC Reliance/Park Royal coaches and 50 Leyland Royal Tigers and Tiger Cubs, with bodies by Alexander, Brush, Roe, Saunders-Roe and Weymann (buses) and by Burlingham and Duple (coaches). Its double-deckers were all Leylands – 24 Titans with Burlingham, Roe and Weymann bodies, and Atlanteans with Alexander and Roe bodies.

No more double-deckers were bought after 1962 as Sunderland District concentrated on full-size single-deckers – Marshall-bodied Reliances and Leopards and Willowbrook Leopards, as well as Plaxton-bodied Leopard coaches.

The Tynemouth & District 1962 fleet was virtually all double-deck, with only two Leopard/Willowbrook single-deckers bought that year. Otherwise it was Guy Arabs with Park Royal, Pickering and Weymann bodies; Leyland Titans with Weymann and Willowbrook bodies; and Roe and Weymann-bodied Atlanteans. Tynemouth went on to buy Daimler Fleetlines with Alexander and Weymann

ABOVE: The majority of the Sunderland District fleet were Leylands; in Sunderland in 1968 is a 1955 Tiger Cub PSUC1/1 with a Weymann 44-seat body, a popular choice for BET companies. The company was unusual among BET fleets with its dark blue livery. *Dale Tringham*

bodies, and Marshall-bodied Leopard buses.

The Gateshead & District fleet was all double-deck with a handful of Guy Arabs with Brush and Weymann bodies and Leyland Titans with Leyland and Weymann bodies. The latest deliveries in 1962 were Atlanteans bodied by Alexander and Roe.

The small Tyneside fleet was all double-deck Leylands in 1962 – Titans with Leyland and Weymann bodies – and the equally small Wakefield's fleet comprised Weymann-bodied Titans, Atlanteans bodied by Roe and Weymann, AEC coaches including Reliances bodied by Burlingham and Weymann, and two remaining AEC/NGT semi-integrals with Beadle coach bodies. Tyneside continued to buy Atlanteans through the 1960s, with Alexander and Weymann bodies, while Wakefield's last deliveries were Plaxton-bodied Bedford SB coaches.

By the end of the 1960s the Northern group of companies had 790 buses, which ranked them seventh in the fleet size stakes of the newly created National Bus Company, below the former BET giants Midland Red, Ribble and Southdown, and former Tilling fleets Crosville, Bristol and United Auto. In 1970 Northern acquired the substantial independent, Venture of Consett, and in 1995 the privatised Go-Ahead Group bought OK of Bishop Auckland.

During the 1970s, under NBC, the various Northern subsidiaries disappeared and a single 'Northern' fleet emerged, but following the sale of the company in 1987 to a management team, local liveries and names reappeared. The privatised Northern company was the foundation of what by 1994 had grown into the Go-Ahead Group, operating bus and rail services throughout England.

New buses bought after the sale of BET to THC continued along existing lines, with further deliveries of Atlantean and Fleetline double-deckers and Leopard and Panther single-deckers, as well as some Fleetline single-deckers. But the NBC influence soon crept in with batches of Bristol/ECW RELLs and the first of what would grow to be a substantial fleet of Leyland Nationals.

ABOVE: In 1958 Sunderland District bought 13 of these Leyland Titan PD3/4s with 73-seat Burlingham bodies. This example is photographed later in its life with the more contemporary fleet-name style. *Stewart J. Brown*

BELOW: The Northern General group of companies was an early customer for Leyland's Atlantean model. This is a Tynemouth & District 1960 PDR1/1 with Metro-Cammell 78-seat bodywork, seen in Newcastle in 1968. *Dale Tringham*

ABOVE: Gateshead & District operated frequent services across the Tyne using high-capacity buses like this Leyland Atlantean PDR1/1 with a Roe 78-seat body, one of 10 delivered in 1960, and seen in Newcastle in 1962. The Gateshead & District livery was changed to green and cream in the 1960s. Behind is a Newcastle Corporation Leyland Titan PD2. *Chris Aston/Omnicolour*

BELOW: Roe-bodied Atlanteans were also supplied to the small Wakefield's fleet in 1962; in North Shields in 1969 this is a 77-seat PDR1/1, complete with the 'Shop at Binns' advert above the destination box, which was so characteristic of Northern General group buses. The Tyne-Tees-Mersey express coach network is advertised on the side. *Dale Tringham*

4 | BET in the North West

Just one BET operator dominated bus services in the North West of England, from the Scottish border right down to Liverpool and Manchester – the mighty Ribble, which ranked second to Midland Red in the BET fleet size stakes. In 1960 Ribble had more than 1,100 buses, and in 1961 this had grown to nearly 1,200. By the end of the decade Ribble was still operating some 1,100 buses and coaches. And there was the North Western Road Car company bridging the gap from Manchester down to the north and east Midlands.

Ribble Motor Services Ltd was set up in 1919 to bring together existing bus operators in the Preston area, and BET's bus arm, BAT, recognised the potential for growth and made a substantial investment in the new company. Like so many of the pioneering bus companies, Ribble expanded naturally and by acquisition, and its operating area grew dramatically in the 1920s and 1930s; by 1938 the fleet had topped 1,000 – only Midland Red and Alexander had larger fleets in the 'company' sector. And in 1938 all of these buses were Leylands, as Ribble supported local industry. Indeed, Leylands would continue to dominate the fleet – apart from wartime Daimlers and Guys and 20 post-war Sentinels – until

the late 1960s, when the Bristol RE became the single-decker of choice, some with Leyland engines, until the inevitable arrival of the Leyland National.

More than half of the 1961 Ribble fleet were double-deckers, all Leylands and mostly Titans of the PD2 and PD3 variety. The PD2s had bodies by Brush, Burlingham, East Lancs, Leyland and Metro-Cammell, and well over half of these had side-gangway lowbridge bodies. Ribble was quick to adopt 30-foot-long double-deckers and developed an attractive forward-entrance style with a full front, built initially by Burlingham and later by Metro-Cammell.

Ribble was, perhaps inevitably given its proximity to the Leyland factory, an early customer for the rear-engined Atlantean double-decker, and took batches in 1959/60, though it did return to Titan PD3s in 1961-63 and bought Leyland Lowlanders in 1964/65, before returning to Atlanteans.

BELOW: The Leyland Tiger Cub was a BET Group staple, and for a short period after this lightweight model was introduced Saunders-Roe bodywork was favoured. Ribble bought 50 with 44-seat bodies in 1954, like this example seen at Whalley in 1966. *Mark Page*

ABOVE: Ribble served the town of Leyland and the great majority of its large fleet was Leyland-built. The Titan was Ribble's standard double-deck model for many years; this PD2/13 has Metro-Cammell 61-seat bodywork and is seen in Preston in 1968. *Dale Tringham*

Among the early Ribble Atlanteans were Weymann-bodied examples fitted out as 50-seat luxury coaches, the 'Gay Hostesses' for the longer-distance express services operated by Ribble and its Standerwick subsidiary company. Acquired in 1932, the Standerwick fleet in 1961 comprised 22 'Gay Hostess' Atlanteans, and 24 Tiger Cub and 36 Royal Tiger coaches.

Ribble continued to champion double-deck coaches, and between 1968 and 1972 bought a fleet of 30 impressive Bristol VRL coaches with 36-foot-long ECW 60-seat coach bodies to replace the Atlanteans.

Coaching was an important part of the Ribble business, with an extensive day and extended tour programme as well as express services linking towns in Ribble territory with centres like Blackpool, Liverpool and Manchester. There were also Yorkshire-Blackpool services, operated jointly with other BET and Tilling companies, and the Lancashire-London services run jointly with Standerwick and Scout Motor Services, a Preston-based company that was acquired by Ribble in 1961, but operated as a separate subsidiary until 1968.

All of this meant that Ribble had a significant coaching fleet. Of its roundly 500 single-deckers in 1961, more than half were coaches – Royal Tigers, Tiger Cubs and Leopards, with bodies by Burlingham, Leyland and Harrington. The single-deck bus fleet included the last 20 front-engined Tigers dating from the early post-war years, the 20 Sentinels, and Leyland Olympics, Royal Tigers and Tiger Cubs with Leyland, Saunders-Roe and Weymann bodies.

During the 1960s Ribble received more of the same. In addition to the Leyland Titans, Lowlanders and Atlanteans, and the Bristol REs, already mentioned, there were substantial deliveries of Leopard buses with Marshall, Weymann and Willowbrook bodies, and Leopard coaches with Duple, Harrington and Plaxton bodies. There were even some lightweight Bedford VAM/Plaxton coaches.

Although Ribble dominated a large part of North West England, it was not the only bus operator by any means. Tilling's Cumberland company served that county, and in Ribble territory there were municipal buses in Accrington, Barrow, Blackburn, Blackpool, Bolton, Burnley (and Colne & Nelson), Bury, Darwen, Haslingden, Lancaster, Leigh, Liverpool, Lytham St Annes, Manchester, Morecambe & Heysham, Oldham, Preston, Ramsbottom, Rawtenstall, Rochdale, St Helens, Salford, Southport,

Warrington, Widnes and Wigan. There were fewer significant independent bus operators in the northern part of the Ribble area, but Bamber Bridge Motor Services was acquired in 1967, and Fishwick of Leyland still survives in private hands. In 1969 Ribble took over United Auto's rather remote Carlisle area services. The major operator in the southern area was Lancashire United, with around 400 buses operating in the area to the west and south-west of Manchester.

In the lead-up to privatisation in the 1980s Ribble's empire was reduced. The north Cumbrian operations passed to NBC's Cumberland company and the Merseyside operations to North Western, but Stagecoach bought both Cumberland and Ribble and so recreated a significant part of the old Ribble empire, although it subsequently sold off some of its Lancashire operations.

The names given to bus companies were often influenced more by history than geography. Thus, although the major operator in North West England was named after the River Ribble that flows from Yorkshire and through Preston, home of the Ribble bus company, the company that adopted the North Western name was based in Cheshire, with operations around Manchester and into Derbyshire.

The North Western company traced its origins to British Automobile Traction services that started in the Macclesfield area in 1913, expanding after the First World War into Buxton and Stockport. The North Western Road Car Co Ltd was formed in 1923 by BAT and Tilling, and in 1930, with a 50% LMS/LNER railway shareholding, it passed into T&BAT (BET and Tilling joint) management, though its vehicle policy was largely Tilling-inspired. It was a surprise, then, when in the 1942 reorganisation it passed into BET control.

Its operating area stretched from the north-east of Manchester deep into Cheshire and Derbyshire, with routes into South Yorkshire and the Potteries. Principal routes included Manchester to Buxton, Glossop and Macclesfield, and a network of routes around Buxton. It was also involved in express services, some jointly with other operators, from Manchester to Derby, Nottingham, Blackpool and North Wales.

The company shared boundaries with a number of important area bus companies – clockwise from Manchester,

BELOW: Ribble turned to the longer PD3/4 Titan model from 1957, with full-fronted forward-entrance bodywork, initially built by Burlingham in Blackpool. This Burlingham PD3 is in Carlisle in 1970, followed by a string of Morris cars. The adverts on either side of the destination display promote Ribble's express services. *Mark Page*

ABOVE: Like many BET fleets, Ribble opted for the longer, heavyweight Leyland Leopard during the 1960s, like this PSU3/1R model with Weymann 45-seat bodywork, one of 60 bought in 1965 and seen in Preston displaying prominent 'Pay as you Enter' signs. It wears the all-red livery that became a feature of several BET fleets. *Mark Page*

BET's Ribble, Hebble, Yorkshire Woollen, Yorkshire Traction, East Midland, Trent and Potteries companies, then Tilling's giant Crosville and lastly the independent Lancashire United. And there were municipal operations at Manchester, Oldham, Rochdale and Stockport.

North Western was a substantial company, with nearly 600 buses in 1960 (roundly 150 double-deck and 450 single-deck), including substantial quantities of Bristols and Leylands. The Bristols were a legacy of its Tilling roots, and included post-war L5G single-deckers and pre-war K5G double-deckers that had been rebodied in the early 1950s. These were withdrawn in the 1960s and replaced by fairly standard BET single-deckers and some more quirky double-deck choices.

Other double-deck buses in the 1960 fleet were rebodied Guy Arabs, early post-war and later Leyland Titans, and a batch of East Lancs-bodied Dennis Lolines. Single-deckers included AEC Reliances and Leyland Royal Tigers and Tiger Cubs, as well as some rare Atkinson Alphas and Albion Aberdonians with Weymann bodies. Weymann and Willowbrook were the favoured bodybuilders for many years, with Alexander bodies becoming more popular during the 1960s.

The buying pattern changed in the 1960s with a move to longer Reliance and Leyland Leopard single-deckers, and for the double-deck fleet more Lolines, some AEC Renowns and, from 1963, Daimler Fleetlines; the latter and many of the Leopards had Alexander bodies. At the end of the decade North Western moved back to Bristol single-deckers, with deliveries of Marshall-bodied RESL and Alexander-bodied RELL buses.

North Western continued to operate some of its coaches in a blue/cream livery, carrying the names of Altrincham Coachways and Melba Motors, businesses that had been acquired in 1958.

Following the creation of Selnec PTE in 1969, responsible for coordinating local bus services within its area, more than half of North Western's local services were in the PTE area, so these passed to the PTE in 1972. Without the busy Manchester area routes the remaining part of North Western's empire was not a viable proposition, so Crosville absorbed the Cheshire operations and Trent the Derbyshire operations. This left North Western as simply a coach operator, and in 1974 the company was renamed National Travel (North West) Ltd.

ABOVE: Ribble was an early Atlantean customer, but reverted to batches of Titan PD3s before returning to Atlanteans in the mid-1960s. Seen in Preston in 1969 is a 1960 Atlantean PDR1/1 with a 72-seat lowheight body by Weymann. All the visible advertising space promotes Ribble leisure products. *Tony Wilson*

BELOW: Ribble was a pioneer of double-deck coaches for longer-distance and interurban work. Between 1959 and 1961 it bought batches of Leyland Atlantean PDR1/1s with luxuriously fitted Weymann 50-seat bodies, like this 1960 example from the associated Standerwick fleet, pausing at Preston in 1968 en route for Morecambe. *Dale Tringham*

ABOVE: The next generation of Standerwick double-deck coaches were 30 impressive 36-foot-long Bristol VRLLH6Ls with 60-seat Eastern Coach Works bodies, used on the longer-distance services that used the growing network of motorways. *Royston Morgan*

LEFT: Many BET companies turned to rebuilding and rebodying buses in the early years after the Second World War, to get extra life out of older buses until new deliveries started to appear. This North Western 1939 Bristol K5G at Northwich in 1962 was one of many rebodied with Willowbrook lowbridge 53-seat bodies in 1951/52. *Martin Llewellyn/ Omnicolour*

ABOVE: With a history of buying Bristol chassis, it was no surprise when North Western bought Bristols after they came back on to the open market. In 1968 it bought 32 of these RESL6Gs with Marshall 45-seat bodies, as seen here in Buxton in 1969 pursued by two splendid Albion Super Reiver tippers. *Royston Morgan*

BELOW: North Western standardised on lowbridge and lowheight double-deckers, and was one of just three BET fleets to buy the Dennis Loline, which was essentially the Bristol Lodekka chassis built under licence. This 1961 Loline III with Alexander 71-seat bodywork is seen at Altrincham in 1971. *Dale Tringham*

ABOVE: After sampling the AEC Renown, North Western turned to the Daimler Fleetline as its standard double-deck model. All had lowheight Alexander D-type 75-seat bodies. This one is in Manchester in 1970. *Dale Tringham*

LEFT: North Western bought 10 unusual buses in 1964 for a route that passed under the 8ft 9in canal bridge at Dunham Massey. They were twin-steer Bedford VAL14s with contour-roofed Strachan 52-seat bodies.
A. M. Davies/Omnicolour

5 | BET in Yorkshire

BET had six bus and coach companies based in Yorkshire in the 1960s. Separated from the rest by Tilling's West Yorkshire company and the independent West Riding was East Yorkshire, based in Hull; to the east of Leeds were Hebble and Yorkshire Woollen, and south-west of them was Yorkshire Traction. Mexborough & Swinton occupied a concentred area around Rawmarsh, Rotherham, Mexborough and Swinton, and there was the specialist coaching company, Sheffield United Tours.

The main centres in Yorkshire also had thriving municipal bus (and tram and trolleybus) fleets, and there were Joint Omnibus Committees, formed when the railway companies bought into existing municipal operations with routes run by outwardly similar fleets, although ownership was shared between the corporations and the railway companies. There were JOCs at Halifax, Huddersfield, Sheffield and Todmorden, and conventional municipal bus operations in areas served by BET operators at Bradford, Doncaster, Kingston-upon-Hull, Leeds and Rotherham (with, in 1960, trolleybuses too at Bradford, Doncaster, Huddersfield, Hull and Rotherham – and trams at Sheffield until October 1960).

East Yorkshire Motor Services Ltd was formed as a bus company by BAT in 1926 to take over two local bus

BELOW: East Yorkshire was one of the small number of BET fleets wearing a blue livery, and the company operated some unusual double-deckers, with normal-height bodywork specially contoured to allow them to pass through the North Bar at Beverley. The fleet also included side-gangway lowbridge buses. This 1956 AEC Regent V MD3RV in Hull in 1970 has 56-seat Willowbrook bodywork to the Beverley Bar style. *Dale Tringham*

operators, and in 1928 passed into T&BAT control; the next year the LNER acquired a shareholding and the company continued to grow. Its operating territory was centred on Hull, with the River Humber as its southern boundary, the North Sea to the east, York and Selby in the west and Malton and Flamborough to the north – though its bus routes reached to Filey and Scarborough in United Auto territory, and to Leeds.

In Hull, East Yorkshire buses ran alongside those of Hull Corporation and it made sense to look at coordinating the services of both operators in the Hull district. A coordination scheme came into effect in June 1934 and, reduced, survived into the 1980s. Under this agreement all revenue earned in the inner part of Hull went to the Corporation while both operators shared revenue taken in an outer zone; in addition, Hull Corporation agreed not to operate outside the coordinated territory.

Leylands were favoured for many years by East Yorkshire, but in the mid-1950s 19 AEC Regent Vs were bought, and AECs would continue to figure in the fleet. The bodies on these Regents remind us of one of the unusual bus designs that will always be associated with the East Yorkshire company. Two of them had conventional lowbridge bodies, but the rest had bodies with an inward taper to the top deck – the Beverley Bar roof contour. This unusual design

allowed full-height double-deckers to pass through the medieval North Bar, the last of Beverley's Gates, erected for tax-collecting purposes, and the only brick-built town gate in the country. A proportion of the East Yorkshire company's double-deckers were built with bodies to the Beverley Bar design, and there were always lowbridge buses for other routes.

The fleet in 1960 stood at 260 buses and coaches, nearly two-thirds of them double-deckers. The oldest buses included wartime Guy Arabs and early post-war Leyland Titan PD1As, as well as Leyland Tiger PS2s and early Royal Tiger buses. There were also AEC Regal III and Regal IV single-deckers acquired with the business of Everingham of Pocklington.

The company continued to buy Leyland single-deckers through the 1960s – Tiger Cub buses and coaches, then Leopards and, interestingly, Panthers and Panther Cubs. The Leopards had bus and dual-purpose-style bodies by Marshall, Weymann and Willowbrook, and coach bodies by Harrington and Plaxton. The rear-engined Panther

BELOW: In 1952 East Yorkshire bought 16 of these Leyland Titan PD2/12s with full-fronted Roe 50-seat coach-seated bodies, to the Beverley Bar outline. They wore the primrose/lighter blue livery used for the coach fleet, and this one is at Bridlington in 1963. *Martin Llewellyn/Omnicolour*

and its smaller-engined brother, the Panther Cub, were less popular choices in BET fleets, but East Yorkshire took Panthers with Marshall and Plaxton bodies, as well as two rare examples with MCW coach bodies; the Panther Cubs had bus bodies by Marshall.

However, East Yorkshire turned right away from Leyland for its double-deck orders, buying AEC Bridgemasters in 1960-63, and Renowns in 1964/65, all with Park Royal bodies. As these were lowheight buses, the Beverley Bar contour was less pronounced. Indeed, the first four were standard Bridgemasters, but later versions had bodies that tapered more gently and had a less pronounced dome. When the company changed to Daimler Fleetlines in 1967 these too had the gentler version of the Beverley Bar taper.

East Yorkshire's bus service network linked Hull with main centres like Bridlington, Goole, Leeds, Scarborough, Selby and Withernsea, and it was one of the operators involved in the Yorkshire Services pool providing express services between London, the West Riding of Yorkshire and the Yorkshire coast. It also had its own seasonal express services linking Hull with Blackpool and Newcastle. The company also offered day tours and extended holiday tours from Hull and other centres in the East Riding.

The East Yorkshire company survives and at the time of writing is one of the two former BET companies that was not acquired by one of the major groups at the time of National Bus Company privatisation and following the subsequent buy-outs. It operates a fleet of more than 300 buses and coaches throughout Hull, East Yorkshire, the North Yorkshire coast and the North York Moors. In North

Yorkshire it trades as Scarborough & District.

The holding company, EYMS Group Limited, owns East Yorkshire Motor Services, Scarborough & District and East Yorkshire Coaches, together with Frodingham Coaches, Manchester-based Finglands Coachways, and Whittle Coach & Bus Ltd, based in Kidderminster.

Two BET companies operated to the west of Leeds. The smaller was Hebble Motor Services Ltd, a company that traces its origins to 1924, operating buses from Halifax to Brighouse and Bingley. Hebble expanded by acquisition and natural growth, and in 1929 the company was acquired by the LMS and LNER companies and agreement was reached with Halifax Corporation to form the Halifax Joint Omnibus Committee, which took over some Hebble routes.

In 1932 BET bought a 50% shareholding in Hebble and the company became increasingly involved in coaching activities. The main bus services linked the main towns of Bingley, Burnley, Bradford, Huddersfield, Leeds and Rochdale. Hebble was part of the Yorkshire-Blackpool Joint Services pool, together with fellow BET companies Ribble, Yorkshire Traction and Yorkshire Woollen, and Tilling's West Yorkshire company.

The 1960 fleet comprised 26 double-deckers, 36 single-deck buses and 32 coaches. The double-deckers were AEC Regents, the single-deck buses Leyland Tigers and Royal Tigers and AEC Reliances, and the coaches were Reliances and Royal Tigers. Bodies for the coaches were built by mainstream companies like Harrington and Plaxton, and more exotic firms like Bellhouse Hartwell. The single-deck buses had Park Royal, Weymann or Willowbrook bodies,

BET BUSES IN THE 1960s

and the Regents had Northern Counties, Metro-Cammell, Roe, Weymann and Willowbrook bodies.

More Regent Vs were bought in the 1960s – with Northern Counties and Weymann bodies – and there were Reliances with Alexander, Harrington, Marshall, Park Royal, Plaxton and Willowbrook bodies. However, increasing number of coaches were also bought – lightweight Thames/Duples in 1961 and Thames/Plaxtons in 1964/65, a little Bedford VAS/Plaxton in 1965, and Reliances with Duple and Plaxton bodies towards the end of the decade.

As part of the NBC's West Riding Group, Hebble's local bus services were transferred to the Halifax JOC in 1971 and it became a coaching company. Hebble became a major part of the new National Travel (North East) in 1974, together with Sheffield United Tours.

Yorkshire Woollen District Transport Ltd was a more typical BET company, with its roots in a BET tramway company designed to serve the Heavy Woollen District of Yorkshire. Motor buses were first introduced in 1913, and between 1932 and 1934 the trams were withdrawn in favour of buses. The LMS and LNER bought a shareholding in the company in 1929.

The Yorkshire Woollen bus routes ran in a tight but populous area bounded by Bradford, Halifax, Huddersfield, Leeds and Wakefield. Many of these routes were jointly operated with fellow BET companies North Western and Yorkshire Traction, with the independent West Riding, and with the Bradford and Leeds corporations and Huddersfield Joint Omnibus Company. Its main high-frequency routes linked Dewsbury to Bradford, Huddersfield and Leeds, and Leeds to Halifax and Huddersfield. It was also a partner in various express service pools – Tyne-Tees-Mersey, Yorkshire-Blackpool, and Yorkshire Services.

The 270 buses in 1960 were roundly 140 double-deckers and 130 single-deckers, the great majority Leylands. There were Tiger, Royal Tiger and the rarer Olympic single-deckers, as well as Titan PD2 and Tiger PS2 double-deckers – the Tigers received new MCW bodies in the mid-1950s. There were also older Guy Arab double-deckers, rebodied in the 1950s, and forward-entrance AEC Regent Vs bought in the late 1950s.

Yorkshire Woollen's other single-deck buses in 1960 were AEC Reliances with Park Royal and Weymann bodies, and there were Reliance/Harrington coaches as well as older Royal Tiger/Windovers, Beadle/Leyland rebuilds and Beadle/Commer integrals.

During the 1960s Yorkshire Woollen bought various double-deck types. First were more AEC Regents, followed by Leyland Titan PD3s, Lowlanders and Atlanteans, and Daimler Fleetlines; the Atlanteans and Fleetlines had Alexander bodies, the Regent Vs Northern Counties bodies, and the Lowlanders Weymann bodies. Single-deck buses were AEC Reliances and increasingly Leyland Leopards; the Leopards had bodies by Marshall and Weymann, and coach bodies by Alexander and Plaxton.

Following the creation of the National Bus Company in 1969 the former BET Hebble and Yorkshire Woollen companies were merged with the West Riding Automobile Co Ltd, the major independent operator that sold out to the Transport Holding Company in 1967, to form the West Riding Group. When NBC was privatised the West Riding Group was sold to its management in 1987 and sold on to

LEFT: An older Beverley Bar Leyland Titan, this 1950 PD2/12 with a Roe 56-seat body is in Bridlington surrounded by British-built cars in 1961. *Martin Llewellyn/ Omnicolour*

British Bus in 1995, which in 1996 was acquired by Cowie and renamed Arriva.

Like Yorkshire Woollen, Yorkshire Traction was not one of BET's glamorous companies, but its buses worked hard in fairly unforgiving urban landscapes and carried large numbers of passengers in a concentrated area. It also had its roots in a tramway company, BET's Barnsley & District, which started running buses in 1913 and became Yorkshire Traction Ltd in 1928, just two years before the last trams ran. The LMS and LNE railway companies bought a shareholding in the company in 1929.

Yorkshire Traction – 'Tracky' – ran a route network that radiated out from Barnsley, towards Doncaster in the east, Rotherham and Sheffield in the south, Huddersfield in the west, and Bradford and Leeds to the north. Although its area was relatively small, it was one of BET's best-performing companies, with such a concentration of industry and associated housing. It was surrounded by other area companies – the independent West Riding and BET's Hebble and Yorkshire Woollen companies to the north, BET's North Western to the west, the Sheffield Joint Omnibus Committee and BET's East Midland company to the south, and Tilling's Lincolnshire Road Car company to the east.

Its buses over the years had mainly been Leylands, and this make represented 87% of its 1960 fleet of 370 buses – 130 double-deckers and 240 single-deckers. There were Tiger, Royal Tiger and Tiger Cub single-deckers, and Tiger, Titan and Atlantean double-deckers; like Yorkshire Woollen it

had rebuilt older Tiger chassis in the 1950s and had new Roe bodies built on them. The non-Leyland buses in the 1960 fleet were rebodied wartime Guy Arab double-deckers, Beadle/Leyland chassisless coaches, and Beadle/Commer single-deck buses.

During the 1960s 'Tracky' virtually bought only Leylands until the end of the decade. It received Tiger Cubs with Alexander and Metro-Cammell bus bodies and Burlingham coach bodies, Leopards with Marshall, Weymann and Willowbrook bus bodies and Plaxton coach bodies, Titan PD3s with Northern Counties and Roe bodies, and Atlanteans with Northern Counties and Willowbrook bodies. In the early 1960s it bought Bedford and Thames coaches, and from 1968 it bought Northern Counties-bodied Daimler Fleetline double-deckers alongside its Atlanteans. It also continued to rebuild early post-war Tiger chassis for rebodying by Northern Counties and Roe, and this practice continued until 1963.

Yorkshire Traction was sold to its management during the NBC privatisation in 1987, and the Yorkshire Traction Group went on to buy up other bus companies – Lincolnshire Road Car and Strathtay Scottish – until it sold out to Stagecoach in 2005.

The Mexborough & Swinton Traction Co Ltd was one of the more unusual BET companies. It started as a tramway system, developed by the National Electric Construction company, in 1907, operating between Rawmarsh, Rotherham, Mexborough and Swinton, and the trolleybuses that started operation in 1915 had replaced the trams by 1929. Motor

ABOVE: In the paler blue coach livery, a 1964 Leyland Leopard PDU3/3R with a Willowbrook 47-seat dual-purpose body is seen at Scarborough. The livery application gives the essentially bus-like straight lines of the BET-style body a suggestion of coach travel. *Royston Morgan*

buses were first introduced in 1922 but the trolleybuses lasted until 1961. In 1931 BET acquired the National Electric Construction company, so Mexborough & Swinton passed into BET ownership. When the last M&S trolleybuses ran in 1961, it marked the end of electric traction in the whole BET Group.

At the start of 1960 the M&S fleet comprised 16 motor buses and 30 trolleybuses. All were single-deckers – Sunbeam/Brush trolleybuses and Leyland Tiger Cub buses and coaches, plus one Ford/Plaxton coach. From 1960 the company received its first double-deckers, Leyland Atlanteans with Weymann bodies, followed in 1964 by a Daimler Fleetline and further Fleetlines in 1969.

In the late 1960s M&S developed a closer relationship with its BET Group neighbour, Yorkshire Traction, and in 1969, following the creation of the National Bus Company, M&S was absorbed by 'Tracky'.

What became Sheffield United Tours Ltd was set up in 1926 as a private transport business, and in 1935 was acquired by the British Automobile Traction company, which continued

the process of buying up other local operators. SUT developed into a significant coach operator, running a programme of day tours and UK and Continental holiday tours. It was also involved in express services between Sheffield and the seaside resorts of Blackpool, Scarborough and Skegness.

The SUT fleet in 1960 comprised roundly 100 coaches, all AECs, with bodies by a range of coachbuilders, famously including the first examples of Plaxton's ground-breaking Panorama design. Added to the fleet in the 1960s were numerous AEC Reliance coaches, with Plaxton bodies, as well as lightweight Bedford and Thames coaches, and a Leyland Leopard.

Following the sale of BET's British bus business to the Transport Holding Company, SUT coaches started to appear in National white livery, and in 1974 the shareholding of the company was transferred to National Travel (North East) Ltd, which ended the company's separate existence.

The SUT name was resurrected in the competitive days of the 1990s as a bus company competing for the local business in and around Sheffield.

ABOVE: At first glance a vehicle type most closely associated with Ribble, this Hebble Leyland Royal Tiger PSU1/15 with a centre-entrance Leyland 41-seat body was one of two new in 1952, and is seen at Halifax in 1965. *Martin Llewellyn/Omnicolour*

BELOW: Sitting in Huddersfield in the November 1969 sunshine, this Hebble AEC Regent V 2LD3RA with a Metro-Cammell 70-seat forward-entrance body was new to Yorkshire Woollen in 1959. The slightly tatty advert promotes coach travel. *H. J. Black*

ABOVE: This well-loaded Hebble AEC Reliance with Alexander Y-type bodywork was photographed in Lichfield in 1968 en route to Cheltenham. *Martin Llewellyn/Omnicolour*

BELOW: Yorkshire Woollen had many of its Leyland Tiger single-deckers rebodied as double-deckers in the post-war years. This was one of six PS2 models that received slightly ungainly Roe 63-seat forward-entrance bodies in 1963, and is seen in Huddersfield in 1972. *H. J. Black*

ABOVE The AEC Regent V was a popular choice for Yorkshire Woollen. This 1961 2D3RA example in Dewsbury in 1969 has 70-seat forward-entrance Northern Counties bodywork. The offside illuminated advertisement panel is out of use. *H. J. Black*

BELOW: Yorkshire Woollen was one of the few BET companies that turned to the Leyland-Albion Lowlander lowheight chassis; this LR7 model in Huddersfield in 1971 has forward-entrance Weymann 72-seat bodywork. *H. J. Black*

ABOVE In the 1960s Yorkshire Woollen bought both Leyland Atlanteans and Daimler Fleetlines. This is an Atlantean PDR1/2, a true lowheight chassis after the semi-lowheight PDR1/1, and has Alexander 75-seat bodywork, one of 12 new in 1967; it is leaving Dewsbury bus station in 1971. *H. J. Black*

BELOW: Yorkshire Traction also had older Leyland Tigers rebodied as double-deckers. This PS2 has 63-seat Roe bodywork and was one of five built in 1961. *Royston Morgan*

ABOVE: Yorkshire Traction was a staunch Leyland supporter; this 1964 Titan PD3A/1 has 73-seat Northern Counties forward-entrance bodywork, and is seen in Huddersfield. Like so many double-deckers in this book, its side advertisement is promoting beer. *Mark Page*

BELOW: The standard Leyland Leopard with BET-style body was bought by many of the BET Group fleets. Yorkshire Traction took nine of these PSU3/4R models with Weymann 53-seat bodies in 1966, as seen in Huddersfield in 1970. *H. J. Black*

ABOVE: Double-deckers with panoramic side windows became fashionable from the mid-1960s, and Yorkshire Traction bought seven of these Leyland Atlantean PDR1/3s with Northern Counties 75-seat bodies in 1969, as seen in Doncaster in that year. *Dale Tringham*

RIGHT: Mexborough & Swinton operated trolleybuses until 1961; the replacement of the trolleybuses by motorbuses in that year marked the end of electric traction in the BET Group. This is a 1948 Sunbeam F4 with a 32-seat Brush centre-entrance body; similar buses were sold to Bradford Corporation when the M&S trolleybuses ceased, and were rebodied as forward-entrance double-deckers.
A. M. Davies/Omnicolour

RIGHT: Leyland Atlanteans were bought to replace the Mexborough & Swinton trolleybuses, like this 1960 PDR1/1 with a Weymann 72-seat semi-lowheight body in Rawmarsh. Note the Maidstone & District-style flash under the windscreens. *Martin Llewellyn/ Omnicolour*

BELOW: Sheffield United Tours was the first customer for Plaxton's ground-breaking Panorama coach body, in 1960. This is the 1960 prototype, a 41-seat coach on an AEC Reliance 2MU3RA chassis, competing in the 1961 coach rally at Brighton. *Royston Morgan*

BET had a virtual monopoly of area bus services in the Midlands, starting with East Midland, Potteries and Trent, and moving south to the giant Midland Red company and its associate, Stratford Blue, which formed a bridge to the South Midlands and the City of Oxford company. To the west were important Tilling Group fleets, Crosville and Bristol Omnibus, and to the east Tilling's Lincolnshire Road Car, Eastern Counties and United Counties companies. And there were municipal operators – Chesterfield in the heart of East Midland territory, Derby and Nottingham in Trent's operating area, and Birmingham, Burton, Coventry, Leicester, Walsall, West Bromwich and Wolverhampton in Midland Red's vast area.

East Midland was a late addition to the BET portfolio. Its roots were in W. T. Underwood Ltd, which started bus services in Derbyshire in the early 1920s. Mr Underwood was a manager with United Automobile Services, at that time based in Lowestoft but with a growing network in North East England. The Derbyshire company continued as a United subsidiary, expanding by acquisition, and was renamed East Midland Motor Services Ltd in 1927 – two years before it was bought by the LMS and LNE railway companies; in 1930 BAT acquired a 51% interest in the business, and in the 1942 reorganisation East Midland became a BET company. In the meantime United Auto had been acquired by T&BAT and the LNER, with its East Anglian operations passing to the new Eastern Counties company with United Auto continuing as a major force in the North East. Both Eastern Counties and United Auto became Tilling Group companies.

East Midland's operating area stretched from Doncaster in the north to Retford on the east, Mansfield in the south and Matlock in the west. Frequent services included the routes linking Chesterfield with Doncaster and Mansfield, and Worksop with Doncaster and Rotherham. There were joint services with BET's North Western and Trent companies, and with several local municipal operators – Chesterfield, Doncaster and Rotherham Corporations and the Sheffield Joint Omnibus Committee. The company also operated seasonal express services linking Chesterfield and other centres with Blackpool, Cleethorpes and Skegness.

With around 220 buses in 1960 – 120 single-deckers and 100 double-deckers – the East Midland fleet was dominated by Leylands, with AEC single-deck buses and coaches, a handful of wartime Guy Arab double-deckers, and three former London Transport RT types acquired with the business of Wass, Mansfield, in 1958.

The East Midland coaches were mainly Leyland Tiger Cubs with Burlingham, Weymann and Willowbrook bodies, together with two AEC Reliance/Weymanns and an ex-Wass AEC Regal IV/Transun.

The oldest single-deck buses were 1949 AEC Regal IIIs with Willowbrook bodies, and the remainder were underfloor-engined models – all-Leyland Royal Tigers, Tiger Cubs with Saunders-Roe, Weymann and Willowbrook bodies, and Weymann-bodied AEC Reliances.

Apart from the Guy Arabs and the RTs, the double-deckers were all Leylands – PD1, PD2 and PD3 Titans with Leyland

LEFT: East Midland bought 15 of these Leyland Tiger Cub PSUC1/1s with Saunders-Roe 44-seat bodies in 1954, and this one is seen against the famous crooked spire of the Parish Church of St Mary and All Saints, Chesterfield, in 1963. *Chris Aston/Omnicolour*

or Weymann bodies, and 20 semi-lowheight Atlantean/ Weymanns bought in 1959/60.

During the 1960s East Midland moved to Leyland's more powerful Leopard model, with bus bodies by Alexander, Marshall and Willowbrook, and coach bodies by Burlingham and Plaxton. It also bought more Reliances – with Alexander, Plaxton and Willowbrook bodies. More Atlanteans followed from 1965, with Alexander bodies, and, more unusually, Albion Lowlanders with Alexander and Metro-Cammell bodies.

In its later years under BET control East Midland moved to rear-engined single-deckers – AEC Swifts with Marshall bodies and ECW-bodied Bristol RELL6Gs.

Following the creation of the National Bus Company, East Midland and the former Tilling fleet, Mansfield District, were placed under common management, and in 1975 Mansfield District was absorbed into East Midland. In 1988 East Midland was bought by its management and in 1989 was sold on by Stagecoach.

Squeezed between Tilling's mighty Crosville company to the west and BET's Midland Red to the south – with BET's North Western and Trent companies to the north and east – Potteries Motor Traction Co Ltd ran intensive services in this industrialised area with, in 1960, a hard-working fleet of around 500 buses. The history of the Potteries company stretched back to the middle of the 19th century when an early horse tramway was opened between Burslem and Hanley, later expanding with the use of steam trams. The system was bought by BET in 1896, becoming Potteries Electric Traction Co in 1898, with the first electric cars running the following year. Motorbuses were tried from 1900 but only really caught on with the more reliable buses available following the First World War.

There was much bus competition in the Potteries area, which led to the replacement of the trams by buses and a change of company name to Potteries Motor Traction Co Ltd – fleet name PMT – to reflect this.

The area continued to be served by many private companies, but PMT gradually acquired most of these, resulting in a very mixed bus fleet. In 1960 this numbered more than 530 – 240 single-deck buses, 40 coaches and 250 double-deckers. The main single-deck type was the AEC Reliance, in bus and coach form, and there were also batches of Albion Aberdonian and Leyland Tiger Cub single-deckers, as well as older front-engined Daimlers, Guys and Leylands. Ninety Leyland Atlanteans dominated the double-deck fleet, with wartime Daimlers and Guys and post-war Leyland Titans, including early examples of the 30-foot-long PD3. There were AEC Regent IIIs and Guy Arab IVs, and, unusually for a BET fleet, there were newer Daimler double-deckers, including a rare CLG5, a batch of 30 CVG5s and a CVD6.30.

During the 1960s the variety in the PMT fleet continued, with double-deckers moving from the Atlantean to the Daimler Fleetline, and single-deck deliveries initially comprising both AEC Reliances and Leyland Leopards, followed, famously, by Daimler Roadliners. The Roadliner was Daimler's first attempt to produce a rear-engined single-deck bus, and although it was an innovative flat-floor chassis, the decision to fit the Cummins V6-200 engine proved to be a mistake. PMT took the prototype bus, and 50 other Cummins-engined buses; these were joined by three Cummins-engined coaches, then, when a Perkins engine was offered, PMT took another 10. With 64 unreliable buses in its fleet, PMT was forced to withdraw them prematurely and

RIGHT: With a fair queue of cars behind it, a 1960 East Midland AEC Reliance 2MU3RA with a 45-seat Weymann body heads past Wardlow Mines on an excursion in 1963. *Martin Llewellyn/Omnicolour*

bought Daimler Fleetline single-deckers and Bristol REs in the early NBC days.

The 12-mile-long urban area that is today's City of Stoke-on-Trent comprises the six towns of Burslem, Fenton, Hanley, Longton, Stoke and Tunstall, and these were the heart of the PMT's high-frequency services in the 1960s, with longer-distance routes reaching out to Birmingham, Buxton, Crewe, Derby, Manchester and Stafford.

PMT was sold to its management in 1986 and in 1994 was bought by First.

Trent Motor Traction Co Ltd started as a bus company in 1913 and grew to serve much of the area around Derby and Nottingham, expanding south to Loughborough and north to Matlock. BAT had an interest from the start, and T&BAT gained control in 1928, the year before the LMS and LNE railways bought a shareholding.

Trent's frequent services included Derby-Alfreton and Nottingham-Mansfield, and there were joint services with fellow BET companies East Midland and North Western, as well as Tilling's Lincolnshire Road Car and Derby Corporation. There were also seasonal express services from Derby and Nottingham to resorts like Blackpool, Cleethorpes, Great Yarmouth and Skegness.

The 1960 Trent fleet of more than 400 buses was fairly evenly divided between single-deckers and double-deckers, and between AECs and Leylands; Loughborough-based Willowbrook supplied more than half of the bodywork.

The oldest buses were AEC Regals and Regents dating from the early post-war years, though Leylands became increasingly popular during the 1950s. There were Royal Tiger and Tiger Cub coaches and buses, Titan PD2 and PD3 models and early Atlanteans.

In the 1960s Trent returned briefly to AEC for Reliance coaches, before standardising on the Leyland Leopard for its single-deck deliveries. Its double-deck choice changed to the Daimler Fleetline from 1963, and in 1967 it was one of the BET companies choosing the now-available Bristol RE/ECW combination.

Trent was sold to its management team in 1986 in the NBC privatisation and went on to buy the important independent, Barton Transport, in 1989, to form trentbarton, still privately owned and one of the best-regarded bus companies in Britain.

The Birmingham & Midland Motor Omnibus Co Ltd – Midland Red – was by far the largest of the BET Group companies in 1960, with more than 1,800 buses and coaches. Among the big company fleets it vied with the Scottish Bus Group's W. Alexander company for top billing in the fleet size stakes, and among the municipal undertakings Birmingham City Transport could field roughly as many buses as either of them – though of course London Transport had four times as many buses as any of them.

Midland Red was a significant operator over a vast area, which covered the counties of Staffordshire, Leicestershire, Warwickshire, Worcestershire, Herefordshire and Shropshire, with routes also stretching beyond these boundaries. It ran literally hundreds of local services, everything from trunk interurban routes to very rural services, and it provided urban services in towns that lacked a municipal bus company, like Hereford, Kidderminster, Malvern, Nuneaton, Rugby, Shrewsbury, Stafford and Worcester. There were also local services in the Birmingham and Leicester areas, complementing the Corporation services.

It was also a major player in long-distance services, some as part of Associated Motorways, other seasonal routes jointly

LEFT: A smartly turned-out standard BET-style Leopard for East Midland – a 1965 PSU3/1R with a 53-seat Willowbrook body at Mansfield depot in 1965.
Chris Aston/Omnicolour

with operators based at the destination resort, and many on its own account, providing limited-stop links between major centres in Midland Red territory. And of course there were the ground-breaking motorway services from Birmingham and Coventry to London, using the newly opened M1 motorway.

Nearly all of these many different types of service were operated by buses and coaches designed and built by the company itself. Apart from batches of AECs, Guys and Leylands bought to help fleet replacement in the decade after the Second World War, and some second-hand acquisitions, the rest of the buses were BMMO types.

The company had first built buses in 1923, and by the 1930s was turning out a range of single-deck buses and coaches, and double-deckers; the majority were for its own use, but some were sold to other fleets, Northern General and Trent being enthusiastic customers.

In the post-war years BMMO types became known for innovation – single-deckers (and later double-deckers) with horizontal underfloor engines; buses with independent suspension, disc brakes and extensive use of glassfibre; and 80mph motorway coaches.

The 1960 fleet comprised roundly 1,000 single-deckers and 800 double-deckers, the current deliveries being C5 family coaches and D9 double-deckers. The C5 coach had first appeared in 1958, sharing a basic common structure with the S14 and S15 buses. A development was the CM5, turbocharged for motorway work, and the CM5T, with toilet. When longer vehicles were permitted, the 36-foot CM6T appeared from 1965.

The D9 followed the in-house D5 and D7 families, but was a 30-foot-long integrally constructed double-decker

with independent front suspension and unusual set-back front wheels. Deliveries started in 1958 and would continue until 1966, by which time Midland Red had turned to Daimler for batches of Alexander-bodied Fleetlines, which would continue to be delivered to the end of the decade. BMMO built two experimental underfloor-engined D10 double-deckers in 1960/61, but this type never went into production – although more than two decades later Leyland, and to a greater degree Volvo, would have success selling double-deckers to this layout.

Midland Red's single-deck bus and dual-purpose vehicles had developed from the ground-breaking underfloor-engined S6 of 1946, with each successive type incorporating innovations and improvements. The newest single-deckers in 1960 were S14 buses and dual-purpose S15s, and from 1962 BMMO built 36-foot-long S16 types, with in-house chassis production ceasing in 1970 with the last S23 type. All of the BMMO-built buses had engines developed by the company, and carried bodies designed by the company but built or completed by mainstream bodybuilders.

As well as the Daimler Fleetlines, Midland Red was casting its net beyond its own BMMO types, and in the 1960s bought several batches of Leyland Leopards with bus and coach bodies.

Under NBC the company was not able to continue to produce its own chassis, but major changes would dilute the proud Midland Red name. In 1973 its local bus services within the West Midlands conurbation were sold to West Midlands PTE, together with more than 400 buses, and while this prompted acquisitions and expansion in its remaining area, in 1981 the rump of Midland Red was divided into five operating

companies – four covering the north (based at Cannock), south (Rugby), east (Leicester) and west (Worcester), as well as a Birmingham-based express company.

The various parts of Midland Red were sold off between 1986 and 1988 in the NBC privatisation. Midland Red North was sold in 1988 to Drawlane, the company that was renamed British Bus in 1992, and was sold to Cowie in 1996, which changed the name to Arriva in 1997. Midland Fox (the renamed East company) was sold first to its management, then to Drawlane in 1989. Midland Red West was sold to Badgerline, which was absorbed into First, and Midland Red South to Western Travel, then to Stagecoach.

Closely associated with Midland Red, but operating as a separate company, was Stratford-upon-Avon Blue Motors Ltd, which had built up a network of local services linking towns like Cheltenham, Evesham, Leamington, Oxford, Stratford and Warwick. Midland Red acquired the company in 1935, but maintained its separate existence and bought proprietary makes of bus and coach rather than inject its own BMMO types.

The Stratford Blue fleet was small, roundly 40 vehicles in 1960, more than half being double-deckers. All were Leylands, Tiger and Tiger Cub buses and Royal Tiger coaches, and Titan double-deckers of PD2 and PD3 varieties. During the 1960s more PD3s were added to the fleet together with Leopard buses and coaches and Atlantean double-deckers, as well as Panther buses, which arrived around the time Stratford Blue was absorbed by Midland Red at the beginning of 1971.

Adjoining both the Midland Red and Stratford Blue operating areas was City of Oxford Motor Services Ltd. Set up in 1906 as City of Oxford Electric Tramways Ltd, by

NEC, it acquired the city's horse trams but opted to develop motorbuses rather than convert the trams to electric traction. City and country services were developed and the company grew quickly in the 1920s and 1930s, particularly following the purchase of a 50% shareholding by the Great Western Railway.

By 1960 the company had grown to some 250 buses, the majority double-deckers, and its operating area stretched through Oxfordshire and into the surrounding counties. As well as the busy urban network in Oxford itself, there were routes to more distant towns like Aylesbury, Newbury, Reading and Swindon, some jointly with other BET and Tilling operators.

The fleet was standardised on AECs, with in 1960 Regals, Reliances and Regents. The Regals were Regal III and Regal IV buses and coaches, and the Regents were Regent III and Regent V models, including many with lowbridge bodies. AEC's monopoly was first broken with the delivery of five Dennis Lolines (with AEC engines), and these would be the first of several batches of lowheight double-deckers. They were followed by batches of AEC Bridgemasters and Renowns, then Daimler Fleetlines towards the end of the decade.

The AEC Reliance was the standard City of Oxford single-decker, with bus, dual-purpose and coach bodies, as well as rear-engined AEC Swifts.

After it became part of NBC, control of another NBC company, the former Tilling-owned South Midland Motor Services Ltd, was passed to City of Oxford; South Midland operated coach tours and holidays, and express services.

City of Oxford was sold to its management in 1987, and in 1994 to the Go-Ahead Group.

ABOVE: Potteries favoured Daimler chassis, unusual among BET companies in the days before the Fleetline; this is a CVG6 with a 63-seat Metro-Cammell Orion body, one of 15 bought in 1956, a batch that included some of the lower-powered CVG5 model. Potteries also operated the prototype Orion body, again on a Daimler chassis. *Mark Page*

BELOW: A Potteries Daimler that remained unique was this impressive 1958 CVD6-30 with a 69-seat Northern Counties body; during its life it received a Leyland 0.600 engine. Its side advert promotes PMT's Coach-Air service to the Isle of Man. *A. Moyes*

ABOVE: The Potteries fleet included a number of buses acquired with businesses it bought, such as this 1957 Leyland Titan PD2/20 with a 55-seat Willowbrook lowbridge body, ex-Baxter, Hanley, in 1958, and seen in Newcastle under Lyme in 1968. *Chris Aston/Omnicolour*

BELOW: Early BET Group 36-foot Leyland Leopards had squarer front and back profiles before the iconic BET-style body evolved. This 1962 Potteries PSU3/3R has older-style Willowbrook 54-seat bodywork, and is seen at Mow Cop. *Martin Llewellyn/Omnicolour*

ABOVE: After trying Leyland Atlanteans, Potteries turned to the Daimler Fleetline; this CRG6LX model has a lowheight Alexander D-type 72-seat body, and was one of 25 delivered in 1964. It is seen at Hanley in 1964. *Martin Llewellyn/Omnicolour*

BELOW: Trent was one of the many BET companies offering extended coach tours. This 1960 AEC Reliance 2MU3RA with a Weymann Fanfare 41-seat body is seen in 1962 at Cranbrook, in Kent. *Martin Llewellyn/Omnicolour*

ABOVE: Trent was another customer for the 36-foot Leyland Leopard with BET-style bodywork. This 1965 PSU3/1R with a Willowbrook 51-seat dual-purpose body in dual-purpose livery, is at Ashbourne in 1972. *Mark Page*

BELOW: Wearing Trent's dual-purpose livery is this 1962 Leyland Tiger Cub PSUC1/1 with 41-seat Alexander bodywork. Alexander had its first serious sales success with this body, built to BET specification. The livery and the chrome embellishments announce that it is a dual-purpose vehicle. *Mark Page*

ABOVE: Trent was an early customer for the Leyland Atlantean, later turning to the Daimler Fleetline. This 1962 Atlantean PDR1/1 with a Weymann 77-seat body, seen at Loughborough, displays the unusual position for the registration plate, a Trent characteristic. *Mark Page*

ABOVE: Although Midland Red built most of its own buses, it turned to outside manufacturers from time to time to ensure that deliveries matched requirements. In 1952/53 it bought 100 Leyland Titan PD2/12s with Leyland 56-seat bodies, and the front end created for these buses became Leyland's standard full-width front. It is seen in Leicester in 1962. *Chris Aston/Omnicolour*

BELOW: The D7 was BMMO's standard own-make double-deck model from 1953 to 1957. Seen in Coventry, with Corporation Daimlers behind, is a 1957 D7 with Metro-Cammell 63-seat bodywork to BMMO design. *Royston Morgan*

LEFT: Newly completed at the Willowbrook coachworks in Loughborough in 1965, this BMMO S17 was one of 100 delivered in 1964/65. The BMMO bodywork was completed by Willowbrook. The S17 was built as Midland Red's standard single-deck bus between 1963 and 1966. *Martin Llewellyn/Omnicolour*

LEFT: Midland Red also bought the Leyland Leopard for bus duties – 100 in 1962/63. This 1963 PSU3/4R has Willowbrook 53-seat bodywork to BET design, and is operating in Leamington Spa in 1965. *Martin Llewellyn/Omnicolour*

LEFT: The D9 was BMMO's own-make double-deck model built from 1958 to 1966, an integrally constructed bus with BMMO bodywork. This is a 1961-built 72-seater in Birmingham in 1964. *Martin Llewellyn/Omnicolour*

ABOVE: In 1960/61 BMMO built two D10 types – underfloor-engined double-deckers – but the design was abandoned. This is the first, built in 1960 with a BMMO 78-seat body, photographed in Stafford in 1969. Volvo and Leyland would later produce underfloor-engined double-deckers with some success. *Dale Tringham*

BELOW: While the BMMO D9 was in production, Midland Red also started to take substantial deliveries of Daimler Fleetlines with Alexander 77-seat bodies; this is a 1967 example. *Stewart J. Brown*

ABOVE: While BMMO built its own coach designs into the mid-1960s, in 1969 it took delivery of 15 Leyland Leopard PSU4A/4Rs with Plaxton Elite 36-seat bodies. *Royston Morgan*

BELOW: Stratford Blue, associated with Midland Red, did not operate BMMO types but bought Leylands instead. These two Titan PD3A/1s with Willowbrook 73-seat forward-entrance bodies, seen in Stratford in 1969, were from a batch of six delivered in 1963. *Dale Tringham*

ABOVE: City of Oxford was an enthusiastic AEC customer. At Gloucester Green, Oxford, in 1968 are a 1960 AEC Regent V MD3RV with a lowbridge East Lancs 58-seat body – the last lowbridge-layout double-deckers supplied to a BET Group fleet – and an AEC Reliance 2MU3RV with a Weymann 44-seat body, also new in 1960. The characteristic 'vee' device took away from the flatness of the front end. *Mark Page*

LEFT: Another Gloucester Green City of Oxford pairing: a 1956 AEC Regent V MD3RV with a Weymann lowbridge 56-seat body, one of seven, and a 1949 AEC Regal III with a 32-seat Willowbrook body, one of 30 delivered in 1949/50 and seen in 1961.
Chris Aston/Omnicolour

ABOVE: This fine line-up is in City of Oxford's Cowley Road Garage in 1970, with AEC Regents, Daimler Fleetlines, an AEC Reliance and a Dennis Loline (fifth from the right). Five Loline IIs with East Lancs bodies were bought in 1961, though they did have AEC engines. *Royston Morgan*

BELOW: City of Oxford stayed loyal to AEC into the rear-engined single-deck era, buying some very early examples of AEC's Swift. This well-loaded example dates from 1967 and is an MP2R model with a Marshall 44-seat body. *Royston Morgan*

BET companies were strong in South Wales, with two significant area operators, South Wales and Western Welsh, as well as the smaller Rhondda, Neath & Cardiff and Thomas Bros companies. Tilling's Red & White company straddled the border with routes centred on the eastern part of South Wales, and reaching over the border to Gloucester and Hereford. Continuing west, Red & White met Western Welsh territory, centred on Cardiff and operating into the valleys, but with more distant territory in West Wales with routes from Carmarthen and to the west coast at St Davids, Cardigan and Aberayron. Another, smaller Tilling company was United Welsh, formed by Red & White in 1938 to bring together operators acquired in the Swansea area. There were also municipal operators in South Wales – at Aberdare, Bedwas & Machen, Caerphilly, Cardiff, Gelligaer, Merthyr Tydfil, Newport, Pontypridd and West Mon; in 1960 Cardiff still operated trolleybuses.

Western Welsh started in 1920 as South Wales Commercial Motors and passed into NEC control in 1927, with the Great Western Railway buying a shareholding in 1929 with a change of the company name to Western Welsh Omnibus Co Ltd. It also ran long-distance services from Cardiff to Carmarthen or Llandrindod Wells and Aberystwyth.

In 1960 Western Welsh had a fleet of nearly 700 vehicles, more than 80% single-deck, reflecting the rural nature of much of its territory outside the Cardiff area. More than

BELOW: Western Welsh built up the largest fleet of Leyland Tiger Cubs in the BET Group, and although most had Weymann bodies there were some other bodybuilders represented, like Willowbrook, which built the 41-seat body on this PSUC1/2, one of 12 delivered in 1961 and photographed in 1969. Tiger Cubs were the company's standard single-deck bus model from 1953 to 1968. *Dale Tringham*

70% of its vehicles were Leylands – Tiger, Olympic, Royal Tiger, Tiger Cub and Olympian single-deckers and Titan and Atlantean double-deckers. Most of the remainder were AECs – Regal III, Regal IV and Reliance single-deckers, and Regent III, Regent V and Bridgemaster double-deckers. There were also Albion Nimbus midi-size single-deckers, and more would be delivered in 1961.

During the 1960s Western Welsh continued to dual-source its requirements from AEC and Leyland, with AEC supplying more Reliances and Regent Vs, together with some Renown lowheight double-deckers, and Leyland providing more Tiger Cubs, plus Leopards, Titans and Atlanteans. The BET Group was a major customer for Leyland's Tiger Cub, and Western Welsh amassed the largest fleet – 271 examples.

Life after BET was not straightforward for Western Welsh. In 1970, under NBC, the Rhondda Transport company was merged with Western Welsh, and in 1972 the West Wales routes were passed to South Wales Transport and to Crosville. This left Western Welsh in its South Wales heartland, and there was further rationalisation when Red & White was merged with Western Welsh and the National Welsh company was formed. Another company in the National Welsh mix was Jones, Aberbeeg, an independent operator that sold out to NBC in 1969.

National Welsh was privatised in 1988 but went into receivership in 1992 following financial difficulties. Much of the business was bought by Stagecoach.

Rhondda Transport Ltd started life as Rhondda Tramways Co Ltd, an electric tramway operator, but the trams had gone by 1934, leaving Rhondda as a motorbus operator. Its compact area was centred on Porth and its 1960 fleet of some 200 buses was dominated by 120 AEC double-deckers, while single-deckers were Leyland Royal Tigers and Tiger Cubs. During the 1960s new deliveries were AEC Regent V double-deckers and Leyland Tiger Cub single-deckers, with Leyland Atlantean deliveries at the end of the decade. The Rhondda company was merged into Western Welsh in 1971.

Linking Cardiff and Swansea by regular express coach services was Neath & Cardiff Luxury Coaches Ltd, with a 1960 fleet of 35 vehicles. All were built to coach specification and the varied fleet included AEC Regal IIIs, Regal IVs and Reliances, and Guy Arab LUFs. During the 1960s N&C received more Reliances, with bodies by Harrington, Duple and Plaxton.

In 1971 Neath & Cardiff passed into the control of South Wales Transport, as did another small BET Group fleet, Thomas Bros (Port Talbot) Ltd; this was set up in 1951 when BET acquired the buses and services of four Port Talbot independents. It owned some 50 buses in 1960 – 38 Leyland Tiger Cub buses with bodywork by

various builders, nine AEC coaches – Regal III, Regal IV and Reliance – and three elderly second-hand open-top double-deckers for seafront services, two AEC Regents and a Bristol K5G.

The Thomas fleet was upgraded in the 1960s with more Tiger Cub buses, Reliances with Marshall and Weymann bus bodies and Harrington and Duple coach bodies.

The other major BET Group fleet in the area was South Wales Transport Ltd, set up by BET in 1914 to feed the group's various tramways in the area. The company also acquired the lease of the famous Swansea & Mumbles Railway, the interurban double-deck tramway, which was not actually acquired until 1959, leading to replacement of the trams by buses in 1960 – arguably the last BET-operated trams, nearly a decade after the last Gateshead trams ran, although there are some who regard it as a railway rather than a tramway. The last of the local Swansea trams had run in 1937, and South Wales Transport grew through acquisition in the 1930s; in 1952 it bought the Llanelly & District company, which ran trolleybuses and motorbuses, though the trolleybuses were quickly withdrawn.

In 1962 South Wales expanded when control of another BET fleet, J. James (Ammanford), was transferred. The company ran intensive urban services in the Swansea, Neath and Llanelly areas, with longer-distance routes to Brecon, Carmarthen and Porthcawl.

The 340-bus fleet in 1960 was 100% AEC, with Regal III and Reliance single-deckers and Regent III, Regent V and Bridgemaster double-deckers. Unusual Regent Vs were two with Roe single-deck bodies for a route in the Llanelly dock area with restricted headroom; six more would follow in 1963. The 1962 acquisition of James brought Leylands into the fleet – Tiger, Olympic, Royal Tiger and Tiger Cub single-deckers and Titan and Atlantean double-deckers, including one of the first prototypes.

The AEC buying pattern continued through the 1960s, with more Reliance buses and coaches, more Regent Vs and Bridgemasters, and the first production Renowns. Three Leyland Leopards arrived in 1963, but these had been ordered by James.

NBC tidied up its companies in South Wales in 1971 and, in addition to the merging of Rhondda into Western Welsh, South Wales Transport took control of the former BET Neath & Cardiff and Thomas Bros companies, and the former Tilling Group United Welsh. This brought great variety into the South Wales fleet, with Bedfords and Bristols from United Welsh, and more Leylands from Thomas Bros.

South Wales Transport was sold to its management in 1987, and in 1990 Badgerline bought the company and its associated Brewers and United Welsh fleets.

LEFT: There were also Tiger Cubs with Marshall bodies in the Western Welsh fleet. This 1963 PSUC1/11 with a 45-seat body is at Brecon in 1972. *Mark Page*

LEFT: Western Welsh also bought AEC Reliances; this 1967 6MU23R example with a Marshall 41-seat dual-purpose body is seen at Cardiff bus station in 1970, wearing the blue/cream coach livery. This batch of buses would be transferred to the South Wales Transport fleet in 1972. *Mark Page*

LEFT: Leyland Atlanteans were bought by Western Welsh from 1960 to 1962, but the company then reverted to front-engined models like the AEC Regent V and Renown and the Leyland Titan PD2, before returning to Atlanteans in 1969. This is a 1960 Atlantean PDR1/1 with a Weymann semi-lowheight 70-seat body. It wears the all-red livery of the time. *Stewart J. Brown*

ABOVE: Two generations of Rhondda double-deckers at Cardiff bus station in 1970 – a 1957 AEC Regent V LD3RA with a Weymann 70-seat forward-entrance body, and a 1969 Leyland Atlantean PDR1A/1 with a Northern Counties 73-seat body. The Atlantean would pass into the enlarged Western Welsh fleet at the end of 1970 with the Rhondda company. *Mark Page*

BELOW: At Cardiff bus station in 1970, preparing to depart on the express service to Swansea, is a 1967 Neath & Cardiff AEC Reliance 6MU4R with a Plaxton Panorama 51-seat body. *Mark Page*

BET BUSES IN THE 1960s

ABOVE: Thomas Bros bought Leyland Tiger Cubs for bus work and AEC Reliances for dual-purpose and coaching duties. This is a 1953 Tiger Cub PSUC1/1 with a Weymann 44-seat body in Port Talbot in 1967. *Chris Aston/Omnicolour*

BELOW: This AEC Reliance 4MU4RA with a Marshall 49-seat dual-purpose body was bought by Thomas Bros in 1963, and is seen in the centre of

RIGHT: South Wales Transport was a good AEC customer, but found itself with Leylands in the fleet following the transfer of the business of fellow BET company, J. James of Ammanford. This is an early Atlantean PDR1/1 with a Weymann 73-seat body, new in 1960. Alongside is one of the three short-lived AEC Swift 2MP2Rs with 48-seat dual-door Willowbrook bodies delivered to South Wales in 1969 but transferred to NBC's new London Country company in 1971.
Royston Morgan

RIGHT: Photographed at the Willowbrook coachworks prior to delivery in 1968 is a new South Wales AEC Reliance 6U2R 53-seater, wearing an experimental livery before the adoption of NBC's standard styles.
Royston Morgan

RIGHT: The AEC Regent was the staple double-decker for South Wales for many years. This 1955 example in Swansea in 1968 is a Regent V MD3RV with a Weymann 59-seat body.
Martin Llewellyn/Omnicolour

BET in the South West | 8

While BET Group fleets were strong in South Wales, the West of England was firmly Tilling Group territory, with the exceptions of the Devon General and Greenslade's companies. The Tilling companies included the closely linked Southern National and Western National companies, the names indicating the areas served by the Southern and Great Western railway companies, which had bought shareholdings in the companies. Sandwiched among them was the Devon General Omnibus & Touring Co Ltd, with its principal bus services radiating out from Exeter to Plymouth, Okehampton, Tiverton, Honiton and Lyme Regis. Devon General buses operated alongside municipal buses in Exeter; in 1947 Devon General and Exeter City Transport had entered an operating agreement, where city buses could be found well away from Exeter and Devon General buses could be found on city services.

The Devon General company was set up in 1919 in Exeter, but in 1922 it was bought by the NEC's Torquay Tramways Co. In 1929 the Great Western and Southern railway companies each bought a share in Devon General and the company came under BET control when NEC was bought in 1931.

The bus fleet in 1960 was around 300 buses, the majority double-deckers. The oldest double-deckers were pre-war AEC Regals that had been rebodied in the 1950s, but there were also Regent III and Regent V types and, from 1959, Leyland Atlanteans. Single-deckers were mainly AECs – Regals and Reliances – with some Leyland Royal Tigers, Beadle-Commer integrals and Albion Nimbus midis.

The Torquay-based Grey Cars business had been bought in 1932 and the name was revived after the Second World War for the Devon General coach fleet; in 1960 this consisted of AEC Regal IV, Reliance and Beadle-Commer vehicles.

Following the BET sale and the creation of the National Bus Company, Exeter Corporation's bus business was sold to NBC and absorbed by Devon General, which in 1971 itself became a subsidiary of Western National. Devon General re-emerged in 1983 when NBC split up the Western National company in advance of privatisation, and in 1986 it was sold to Transit Holdings, which itself was bought by Stagecoach in 1996.

The Greenslade family started out in coaching in 1912, and in 1933 formed Greenslade's Tours Ltd. The company had also started local bus services, but these were sold to Devon General in 1948. In 1953 BET bought the coach business, which expanded by acquisition. By 1960 the company had some 80 coaches, AECs and Bedfords; it continued to buy AEC Reliances during the 1960s, as well as some lighter-weight Thames Traders.

The Grey Cars fleet was merged with Greenslade's in 1971, and the Greenslade's business passed to National Travel (South West) in 1973.

LEFT: Devon General was one of BET's AEC fleets; this 1956 Regent V MD3RV with a Metro-Cammell 59-seat body is at Torquay in 1961. *Royston Morgan*

ABOVE: The conductor stands proudly beside his 1965 Devon General AEC Regent V 2MD3RA with its forward-entrance Willowbrook 59-seat body at Exmouth. *Peter G. Smith/Omnicolour*

BELOW: Beside the water at Torquay in 1966 is a newly delivered Devon General AEC Regent V 2D3RA with a 59-seat Metro-Cammell body. *Royston Morgan*

ABOVE: Among Devon General's 1965 deliveries was this AEC Reliance 2MU3RA with a 41-seat Park Royal body, seen at Exeter in 1969. *Royston Morgan*

BELOW: AEC's monopoly of the Devon General double-deck fleet was broken by the arrival of Leyland Atlanteans from 1959, including nine of these 'Sea Dog' convertible open-toppers with Metro-Cammell 75-seat bodies. All were named after famous seafarers – this is 'Earl Howe', skirting the sea at Torquay in 1970. *A. M. Davies/Omnicolour*

ABOVE: Two Harrington Grenadier 41-seat coach-bodied AEC Reliance 2MU4RAs from Devon General's associated Greenslade's fleet are seen at Exeter in 1969. *Royston Morgan*

BELOW: This Grey Cars AEC Reliance 2MU3RV with a Willowbrook Viscount 41-seat coach body, new in 1961, is seen at Newton Abbot in 1964. On the left is a 1952 Devon General AEC Regent III with an early style of 'new-look' front and Weymann Aurora bodywork. On the right is an earlier bus from the same batch with a more conventional appearance. *Royston Morgan*

BET BUSES IN THE 1960s

Around the vast area that was covered by London Transport – and in 1960 it stretched from Luton in the north to Horsham in the south, and from High Wycombe in the west to Gravesend in the east – were territorial operators, often working into the LT area from outside. To the east, north of the Thames, was the Tilling Group's Eastern National company, and directly north was United Counties, again Tilling. To the west was Tilling's Thames Valley, and to the south-west was BET's Aldershot & District. Continuing round the south of LT's area were two more BET companies, Southdown and Maidstone & District, and to the east of Maidstone & District was BET's East Kent.

Two small London-based coach companies owned by BET were Blue Cars Continental Coach Cruises Ltd, and Red Line Continental Motorways Ltd. The Blue Cars fleet of 32 coaches was dominated by Leylands with Bellhouse Hartwell

bodies, although there were also left-hand-drive coaches based on the continent. Red Line had just six coaches, mainly AECs with Windover or Strachan bodies.

The Aldershot & District Traction Co Ltd was formed by the BAT group in 1912 to acquire pioneering operators in the Aldershot and Farnborough areas, and to grow by steady acquisition. In 1928 A&D passed into T&BAT control, and in 1930 the Southern Railway took a shareholding in the company. BAT had also started bus operations in Reading, and these became the basis for another area bus company, Thames Valley. Like A&D it passed to T&BAT in 1928, but in the 1942 reorganisation it passed into Tilling control.

BELOW: This 1957 Aldershot & District AEC Reliance MU3RV with a Weymann 43-seat body is at Aldershot in 1968. *Dale Tringham*

Aldershot & District operated in an area bounded by Horsham, Guildford, Reading and Winchester, and in addition to frequent local services it ran limited-stop services to London as well as seasonal services to South Coast resorts. Although there were no municipal operators in A&D territory, it met Reading Corporation buses on its regular services.

A feature of the A&D fleet over the years was the number of Guildford-built Dennis chassis it bought, and the 1960 fleet of 340 buses included more than 200 Dennises, as well as AECs and Guys. Dennis models included Falcon and Lancet single-deckers and Lance and Loline double-deckers. The newer single-deckers were AEC Reliances with bus and dual-purpose bodies. The Guys were wartime chassis with newer double-deck bodies.

Deliveries during the 1960s were more Lolines and Reliances, with bodywork by Alexander and Weymann on the Lolines, and Duple, Marshall, Metro-Cammell, Park Royal, Weymann and Willowbrook on the Reliances.

Following the creation of NBC, Aldershot & District and Thames Valley were brought together as the Thames Valley & Aldershot Omnibus Co Ltd, with the fleet name Alder Valley. In 1986 Alder Valley was split into two – Alder Valley North and Alder Valley South – in preparation for the privatisation of NBC. The North company was sold to Q Drive, operating as Bee Line; South was sold to Frontsource, which shortly sold out to Q Drive, reuniting the two parts

of the company. Changes of ownership and the selling off of parts of the company led to what was left of the former Alder Valley territory passing into the hands of First (in the northern part) and Stagecoach (the southern part).

Stretching along the South Coast between Portsmouth and Eastbourne, Southdown was always one of Britain's most charismatic bus companies. Its roots were in pioneering horsebus and motorbus companies in the Brighton and Worthing areas, which came together in 1915 under the new Southdown Motor Services Ltd, and after the First World War the company set about expanding its territory by organic growth and acquisition. It also started express services to London from its main South Coast centres. Coaching was important to Southdown, and comprehensive day and extended tour programmes were developed.

In 1928 Southdown became a T&BAT subsidiary and the Southern Railway bought a shareholding two years later. In 1942 it passed to BET.

Southdown's bus services operated in and around the Sussex coast, and inland to Horsham, Lewes, Petersfield and Uckfield; there were also the important express services to London from a range of towns, and involvement with other

BELOW: A newer Aldershot & District Reliance, a 1968 6U3ZR model with a dual-purpose BET-style Willowbrook 51-seat body, is also seen at Aldershot in 1968. *Dale Tringham*

operators in the South Coast Express service linking Margate with Bournemouth.

There were other operators in Southdown territory, notably Tilling's Brighton Hove & District, municipal operations at Brighton, Eastbourne and Portsmouth – with trolleybuses still running at Brighton and Portsmouth in 1960 – and a significant private operator in Provincial, linking Gosport and Fareham.

By 1960 the company operated just under 1,000 vehicles, fairly evenly split between single-deckers and double-deckers. More than 800 of the fleet were Leylands, with more than 100 Guys as well as smaller quantities of other types, including Commers and Beadle-Commers.

The Leyland single-deck fleet comprised Tigers, Royal Tigers and Tiger Cubs, and the majority of these carried coach bodies – more than 300 of them. There were also Beadle semi-chassisless single-deck coaches and buses built in the early 1950s from pre-war Tiger TS8s.

The Leyland double-deck fleet included late pre-war Titan TD5s with post-war bodies, and examples of the Titan PD1, PD2 and PD3, including the first batches of the famous Northern Counties-bodied PD3 'Queen Marys'.

Southdown's Guys were utility Arabs with closed-top and open-top bodies, and the company bought more double-deck Arabs in 1948 and in the mid-1950s.

In addition to the Beadle rebuilds there were integral Beadle-Commer coaches, as well as Commers with Burlingham and Harrington coach bodies.

Deliveries of 'Queen Mary' PD3s continued through the 1960s to 1967 as the company resisted the lure of rear-engined double-deckers, but with PD3s no longer available it turned to Daimler Fleetlines in 1970. At the same time it

continued to buy Tiger Cub buses and coaches before turning to Leyland's more powerful Leopard for both coach and bus duties. There was another move away from Leylands when it bought Bristol RESL buses in 1968.

When the National Bus Company was formed in 1969 the former Tilling Group company, Brighton Hove & District, was placed under Southdown control, but prior to privatisation the Brighton & Hove operations became a separate company again. Southdown was sold to its management in 1987 and was sold on to Stagecoach two years later.

Bounded by Southdown, London Transport and East Kent, Maidstone & District Motor Services Ltd was set up in 1911 to acquire services started in 1908 from Maidstone to Chatham and Gravesend. Like Southdown, BAT had an interest in M&D, and the Southern Railway took a shareholding in 1930. It grew in the 1920s and 1930s by acquiring other local bus operators and replacing the Chatham trams. It bought the trolleybus-operating Hastings Tramways Co in 1935 and this continued as a separate company until 1957; the trolleybuses were replaced by motorbuses in 1959. Trolleybuses still operated in M&D territory, with Maidstone Corporation. M&D passed to BET in 1942.

M&D's territory met with London Transport at places like East Grinstead, Gravesend and Sevenoaks; with Southdown at Crowborough and Pevensey; and with East Kent at Ashford and Faversham. Its long-distance services linked main points in West Kent with London, and there were seasonal services to coastal resorts on the South Coast.

Just over half of the 1960 M&D fleet of just under 800 vehicles were double-deckers, and nearly half of the double-deckers were Bristols; unusually for a BET company, M&D bought Bristols in the early post-war years. There were also

AEC Regent Vs, rebodied wartime Daimlers, rebodied wartime and post-war Guys, and Leyland Titan PD2s and early Atlanteans.

The single-deck bus fleet was dominated by AEC Reliances, and there were Beadle/AEC rebuilds, Bristols, Dennis Falcons, Harrington-Commer integrals and a unique Saro integral.

M&D's heavy coach commitment meant that there were more than 200 coaches, mostly AEC Regals and Reliances, as well as Beadle/AEC and Beadle/Leyland rebuilds, Harrington-Commer integrals, Leyland Tigers and Royal Tigers, and a luxury Cr Avenger. Many of the single-deck buses and coaches had bodies by Harrington, built along the coast at Hove.

During the 1960s more Atlanteans and Reliances followed, but from 1963 the company switched to the Daimler Fleetline for its double-deck needs. There would also be Albion Nimbuses for rural work, and in the late 1960s M&D received batches of rear-engined Leyland Panther single-deckers.

M&D was sold to its management in 1986 but was sold on in 1994 to British Bus, itself soon to be taken over by Cowie and rebranded as Arriva.

The early history of East Kent reflects the pattern at Southdown and Maidstone & District, where local companies were amalgamated – in this case in 1916 as East Kent Road Car Co Ltd. It became part of the T&BAT group in 1928, got railway involvement from 1930 when the Southern took a shareholding, and in 1942 passed to BET.

Like its BET neighbours to the west, East Kent had a large coach fleet – nearly one-third of its 630-plus vehicles – and there were nearly twice as many double-deck as single-deck buses. Its area was bounded by the sea to the east, and by Maidstone & District to the west, with boundary towns at Ashford, Faversham, Hastings and Rye. In addition to its local bus network, the company ran express services from points in Kent to London.

The 1960 fleet comprised AEC and Dennis single-deck buses, AEC, Guy and Leyland double-deckers, and coaches from a variety of manufacturers – AEC, Bedford, Beadle, Commer, Dennis, Leyland and Thames.

Dennis and Leyland single-deckers had been popular in the early post-war years, but East Kent was moving towards the AEC Reliance. For double-deckers the company had favoured Leylands, but moved on to Guy before switching to AEC in 1959.

Further batches of AEC Regent V double-deckers joined the fleet during the 1960s, as well as three Bridgemasters and more Reliance buses and coaches. With Regent Vs no longer available, East Kent bought Daimler Fleetlines in 1969.

In 1987 East Kent was sold to its management team, passing in 1993 to Stagecoach.

BELOW: Southdown favoured Leylands, like this 1955 Tiger Cub PSUC1/1 with a 39-seat Park Royal body, here operating as a one-man bus at Worthing in 1970. *Dale Tringham*

ABOVE: This smartly presented 1956 Leyland Titan PD2/12 with a 59-seat East Lancs body wears the attractive Southdown livery well, as seen at Tunbridge Wells in 1969. *Dale Tringham*

BELOW: As well as Leylands, Southdown bought Commers for its coaching fleet. This is a Beadle-Commer integral 41-seater, one of 20 bought in 1957 and seen at Brighton in 1968. *Dale Tringham*

ABOVE: From 1958 Southdown standardised its double-deck fleet on Leyland Titan PD3/4s with 69-seat full-fronted Northern Counties bodies – the iconic 'Queen Marys'. This is one of the first batch from 1958, at Rottingdean 10 years later. *Dale Tringham*

BELOW: Southdown was a good customer for Northern Counties, which bodied 30 of these unusual Leyland Leopard PSU3/1Rs in 1969, as seen at Brighton in 1970. *Dale Tringham*

BET BUSES IN THE 1960s

ABOVE: In 1968 Southdown took delivery of 40 Bristol RESL6Gs with 45-seat Marshall bodies; this one is at Petworth in 1971. *Mark Page*

BELOW: BET's South Coast fleets were heavily involved in coaching work, and this one, seen at Hastings in 1972, is a Maidstone & District AEC Reliance 2MU3RV with a 37-seat Harrington Cavalier body, from a batch of 10 delivered in 1962. *Dale Tringham*

ABOVE: Maidstone & District was one of the first customers for the Leyland Atlantean, but switched to the Daimler Fleetline in the 1960s. This 1962 Atlantean PDR1/1 has Weymann 77-seat bodywork and is at Hastings in 1968. *Dale Tringham*

BELOW: This later Maidstone & District coach is one of 12 Leyland Leopard PSU3A/4RTs with Duple Commander 45-seat bodies, delivered in 1968. *Royston Morgan*

ABOVE: Two of East Kent's many AECs, these are a 1955 Reliance MU3RV with a dual-purpose Weymann 41-seat body and, in the background, a Regent V 2D3RA with a Park Royal 72-seat forward-entrance body, new in 1964. *Royston Morgan*

BELOW: Like Ribble and Southdown, East Kent went for 30-foot-long full-fronted forward-entrance double-deckers, but chose the AEC Regent V rather than the Leyland Titan PD3. One of the first batch of 40, a 1958 LD3RA with a 72-seat Park Royal body, is at Rye in 1972. *Dale Tringham*

ABOVE: Later East Kent Reliances were 36-foot models; this is a 1963 2U3RA with a 49-seat Park Royal coach body, in London in 1973. The following year this chassis would be rebodied with a new Plaxton coach body. *Stewart J. Brown*

BELOW: Although East Kent is probably most fondly remembered for its full-fronted Park Royal-bodied AEC Regent V fleet, it also received more conventional halfcab versions in 1963-66; this 1964 Regent V 2D3RA with 72-seat forward entrance Park Royal body is at Dover Marine Station on a wet day in June 1969. *Mark Page*

Jointly owned companies | 10

BET and its constituents had interests in a number of bus and coach companies jointly with others under different ownership. These were mainly coaching companies and the creation of the National Bus Company made the question of ownership much easier.

Associated Motorways was set up in 1934 to strengthen the existing Black & White company with financial interests from a number of the major company fleets. Operating as Black & White, and based at Cheltenham, a significant network of coach services linked the Midlands with South West England, and London with South Wales, using Cheltenham as a hub that provided a wide range of interchange facilities.

By 1960 Associated Motorways was owned jointly by BET's Midland Red and Tilling's Bristol Omnibus, Eastern Counties, Lincolnshire, Red & White, Royal Blue and United Counties companies. Black & White Motorways Ltd, which was owned by Bristol Omnibus, Midland Red and City of Oxford, ran 100 coaches in 1960, comprising AECs, Bristols, Guys and Leylands. The Bristols were Duple-bodied L5G models dating from 1949, and these were followed by Willowbrook-bodied Leyland

Royal Tigers, Duple and Willowbrook-bodied Guy Arab LUFs, and Duple, Roe and Willowbrook-bodied AEC Reliances. Deliveries during the 1960s included more AEC Reliances, batches of Leyland Leopards and Daimler Roadliners.

Black & White formed the nucleus of National Travel (South West), set up in 1973 by NBC, and also taking in BET's Greenslade's operation.

County Motors (Lepton) Ltd was formed in 1927 by the Yorkshire Traction and Yorkshire Woollen companies and the independent West Riding company, to acquire bus services in the Barnsley, Dewsbury, Huddersfield and Wakefield areas, and the fleet was largely influenced by Yorkshire Traction's buying policies for single-deckers

BELOW: County Motors was jointly owned by BET's Yorkshire Traction and Yorkshire Woollen companies, and the then independent West Riding. The fleet largely followed Yorkshire Traction's buying policy for single-deckers and West Riding's for double-deckers; this Leyland Leopard PSU3/1R with a 54-seat Willowbrook body was one of two delivered in 1962, and is seen in Huddersfield in 1965. *Chris Aston/Omnicolour*

RIGHT : Black & White bought 24 of these Leyland Leopard PSU3/3R with Plaxton Panorama 47-seat bodies between 1962 and 1964. This one is sitting at Victoria Coach Station, London when new in the company of an East Kent AEC Reliance and a Standerwick Leyland Atlantean 'Gay Hostess'. *Photobus*

and West Riding's for double-deckers. The fleet in 1960 comprised 17 double-deckers, six single-deck buses and two coaches. Double-deckers were rebodied wartime Guy Arabs and post-war Arabs and Wulfrunians; single-deck buses were Leyland Tiger Cubs, and the coaches were Windover-bodied Leyland Tiger PS2s. During the 1960s Leyland Leopards and Titan PD3s were added to the fleet.

A. Timpson & Sons was a major London area coach operator, jointly owned by BET and the British Transport Commission. Timpson's grew as a private operator in the 1920s and 1930s, and on the death of the owner BET and Tilling acquired the business. In 1960 the fleet of 120 coaches operated seasonal services from London to seaside resorts as far apart as Great Yarmouth and Paignton, as well as private

hire and excursion work. Most of the Timpson coaches were AECs, Regal IVs and Reliances, as well as lighter-weight Commers and Fords.

Timpson's, together with the formerly BTC-owned Tilling's Transport and Samuelson New Transport, owned by London Coastal Coaches, were the basis for the new National Travel (South East) company in 1974, later renamed National Travel (London).

BELOW: County Motors was amalgamated into the Yorkshire Traction company in 1969, and seen here in Huddersfield in 1973, in the livery of its new owners, is this ex-County 1963 Leyland Leopard PSU3/1R with a 53-seat Willowbrook body. *H. J. Black*

BET after NBC | 11

At first the formation of the National Bus Company in 1969 had little obvious external effect on the buses and coaches operated by the former BET Group companies, as they continued to trade as normal, and received new vehicles that had been ordered before the sale of BET's British bus interests to the Transport Holding Company, which paved the way for the massive group that covered much of England and Wales.

But it was clear that this situation would not be allowed to continue. The patchwork of company operating areas meant that there was some duplication and overlap, and it made sense to NBC to tidy up some of the anomalies that existed now that once-separate companies found themselves under common ownership.

A start was made in 1969 when Ribble acquired the Carlisle area services of the former Tilling Group United Auto company, Yorkshire Traction absorbed the County Motors and Mexborough & Swinton businesses, and the former Tilling Brighton Hove & District company passed into Southdown control.

From 1970, as NBC got to grips with its vast empire, the changes came thick and fast. In that year Devon General passed into the control of the former Tilling Western National company, and Hebble became Yorkshire Woollen's coaching unit. There were also acquisitions in 1970 – the independent Venture Transport passed to Northern General, and Exeter Corporation sold out and Devon General took over.

The situation in South Wales was tidied up in 1971 when South Wales Transport acquired its BET neighbours, Neath & Cardiff and Thomas Bros, as well as Tilling's former United Welsh business. The same year Rhondda passed to Western Welsh control, Stratford Blue was fully absorbed by Midland Red, the former Tilling South Midland coaching business passed from Thames Valley to City of Oxford, and in Devon Grey Cars merged with Greenslade's.

BELOW: The rationalisation that followed the bringing together of the former BET and Tilling empires under National Bus Company control led to some unusual sights. When Ribble took over United Auto's isolated Carlisle outpost in 1969 it acquired distinctly non-Ribble vehicles like this 1961 Bristol MW5G with an ECW 45-seat body, seen at Carlisle in 1969. *Dale Tringham*

BET BUSES IN THE 1960s

In 1972 the former Tilling Midland General business passed into Trent control, while the management of Mansfield District passed to East Midland; Aldershot & District was merged with Tilling's Thames Valley to create the Alder Valley company; North Western's operations in Greater Manchester passed to Selnec PTE, while the rest of its bus services passed to Crosville and Trent; and South Wales Transport took over Western Welsh's Neath and Haverfordwest depots.

National's coaching operations were rationalised in 1973/74 with the creation of the National Travel companies, and former BET companies found themselves subsumed into – or indeed renamed as – NBC's new National Travel coaching unit. National Travel (North East) combined the coaching activities of Hebble and Sheffield United Tours; National Travel (North West) brought together the coaching interests of North Western and Standerwick; National Travel (South West) combined Black & White, Greenslade's and Shamrock & Rambler; National Travel (Midlands) was created from acquired companies; and National Travel (South East) was formed from the Tillings Transport, Timpson and Samuelson businesses.

For many observers, one of the saddest consequences of BET's absorption into NBC was the disappearance of much-loved liveries. BET's fairly relaxed attitude to corporate identities was very different from Tilling's, where the majority of the fleets wore either Tilling Red or Tilling Green colours, with cream relief, on buses that were themselves highly standardised, as a result of the Bristol/ECW in-house connection. Neither BET nor Tilling felt it necessary to remind passengers of their existence on their buses.

So while Tilling buses were usually red or green, BET buses were usually red, or green, or blue. Shades of red were by far the most popular main colours – for 18 of the BET bus companies – with green next (just five), then blue (just four). Then there were the brown/red Neath & Cardiff 'brown bomber' coaches, and the impressive maroon/red/duck-egg green of City of Oxford. And even the 'red' fleets varied in shade and application so that buses of individual operators could be quickly recognised. With the arrival of spray painting, some companies opted for the simple life and went for all-over red, which could look rather drab. Others took a greater pride in the appearance of their vehicles, and used cream relief to good effect. And of course there were the distinctive fleet names – the swoops and swirls of Aldershot & District and Maidstone & District, and the confident Ribble and Southdown names.

At first the existing liveries survived the formation of NBC, but a corporate style was on the horizon, so traditional fleet

BELOW: Unable to buy any more Leyland PD3 'Queen Marys', Southdown briefly turned to the Daimler Fleetline for its double-deck requirements, later taking Bristol VRT and Leyland Atlantean deliveries. At Worthing on its first day in service in 1971 is one of 15 CRG6LX Fleetlines bought in 1970/71 with Northern Counties 71-seat bodies. *Dale Tringham*

ABOVE: Under NBC, Devon General was absorbed into the former Tilling Western National company in 1971, running for some time with Devon General fleet names in NBC poppy red, but Western National's leaf green was later adopted. At Torquay in 1985 are red and green Devon General Bristol VRTSL6Gs with 74-seat ECW bodies. *Gavin Booth*

names were replaced by National's double-N logo and block capitals, then the old colours were replaced by poppy red, leaf green and blue. NBC blue was short-lived, but the red and green liveries – relieved by white, but not always – gradually took over. The BET fleets that had been 'red' fleets normally stayed red – though East Midland went green, and Alder Valley went with Thames Valley's previous colour rather than Aldershot & District's green. Of the BET 'blue' fleets, East Yorkshire soon became red, while Sunderland District and Thomas Bros were absorbed into Northern General and South Wales Transport respectively, and their buses became red.

NBC also adopted a Tilling-like approach to vehicle buying. It saw merit in reducing the many different types of chassis and body that it inherited, the greatest variety being from BET fleets. It still had the stake in Bristol and ECW that was inherited from the Transport Holding Company, but this had been reduced when Leyland took a 25% shareholding in Bristol and ECW, which released their products back on to the open market. Leyland increased its shareholding to 50%, so that NBC inherited the balance. Leyland and NBC formed a joint venture in 1969 to build the Leyland National single-deck citybus, which was launched in 1970 and was clearly going to feature in NBC orders for years to come.

There was also the Bristol VRT rear-engined chassis, usually with ECW bodywork, which was becoming the standard Tilling double-deck model at the time NBC was formed. It seemed inevitable that the National and the VRT would become NBC's standard models, with odd batches of more specialised types to add variety.

In practice, the Leyland National was not available as quickly as NBC might have liked, and the general introduction of New Bus Grants, to encourage UK operators to buy new buses, was putting a strain on the resources of NBC's 'in-house' suppliers. This meant that many former BET companies continued to receive the type of bus that they had previously had, and probably the types they would have chosen, given a free hand. So although in many NBC fleets the National and VRT were indeed standard fare, there were still significant batches of other makes going into service into the 1970s.

It was 'business as usual' for single-deck deliveries to most of the former BET fleets. The tried and trusted Leyland Leopard with bus or dual-purpose bodywork from Alexander, Marshall and Willowbrook continued to enter service in significant quantities with fleets like East Yorkshire, Midland Red, Trent, Western Welsh, Yorkshire Traction and Yorkshire Woollen. AEC Reliances with similar bodies went to Alder Valley, Devon General, City of Oxford and South Wales. The Leopard was also a popular choice for coaching work, and Duple, Plaxton and Willowbrook-

ABOVE: Following the break-up of the Sheffield Joint Omnibus Committee in 1970, the Yorkshire Woollen fleet was boosted with double-deckers including rare Leyland Titan PD2/20s with ECW 59-seat bodies, a unique combination that was only possible because of the railway interest in the JOC. *Dale Tringham*

bodied examples were supplied well into the 1970s. 'AEC' fleets continued to receive Reliance coaches with Duple or Plaxton bodies.

Some BET companies had turned to rear-engined single-deckers, and the single-deck version of the Daimler Fleetline was bought by companies like Maidstone & District, Northern General, City of Oxford, Potteries and Yorkshire Traction. East Kent received Alexander-bodied AEC Swifts, and quite a number turned to the Tilling Group's favoured Bristol RE. Some BET companies had chosen the RE in the days before NBC, but more turned to what many believed was the best of the first-generation rear-engined single-deckers. The RELL with ECW bodywork went to companies like Alder Valley, East Midland, Northern General, Potteries and Trent; RELLs with Marshall bodies went to East Midland, Ribble, South Wales, Southdown and Trent; and RELLs with Alexander bodies went to North Western.

There was also a move to lighter-weight single-deck buses for more rural operations, and Alder Valley, Midland Red and City of Oxford opted for Fords, while South Wales chose Bedfords. Bristol's LH was bought in short LHS form by Devon General, East Yorkshire, Western Welsh and Trent, and in LH form by Devon General, East Kent and Trent.

The hunger for new double-deckers meant that the former BET fleets were able to continue taking deliveries of their favoured Daimlers and Leylands rather than the Bristol

VRT model that would eventually become the principal NBC 'choice'. So Leyland PDR1 Atlanteans were delivered to East Midland, East Yorkshire and Western Welsh with Alexander bodies, and to Maidstone & District with Metro-Cammell bodies; the improved AN68 Atlantean went to East Yorkshire, Northern General, Ribble, Southdown and Yorkshire Woollen with Park Royal-Roe bodies, to East Kent, Northern General, Ribble and Trent with ECW bodies, and to Trent with Willowbrook bodies.

Daimler Fleetlines were built for East Yorkshire, Midland Red, Northern General, City of Oxford, Trent and Yorkshire Woollen with Alexander bodies, for Southdown, Trent and Yorkshire Woollen with ECW bodies, and for City of Oxford and Southdown with Northern Counties bodies.

However, eventually supply caught up with demand and the ECW-bodied Bristol VRT joined virtually every former BET fleet, as did the ubiquitous Leyland National, and the last vestiges of BET's former individuality disappeared into the NBC corporate pot.

ABOVE: The Rhondda company was absorbed into Western Welsh in 1970, although the fleet name lived on. This 1971 Leyland Atlantean PDR1A/1 with a 73-seat Alexander body was one of nine ordered by Rhondda but delivered to Western Welsh. *Stewart J. Brown*

BELOW: After years of separate existence, Stratford Blue was merged into its parent company, Midland Red, in 1971, bringing some non-standard buses into the main fleet, like this 1962 Leyland Titan PD3/4 with a 73-seat Northern Counties forward-entrance body. *Dale Tringham*

RIGHT: City of Oxford received Stratford Blue 1967 Leyland Atlantean PDR1A/1s with Northern Counties 75-seat bodies via Midland Red in 1971, when this one was photographed in Oxford. They had been the last new double-deckers for the Stratford Blue fleet. *Dale Tringham*

BELOW: In 1972 NBC merged Aldershot & District with its former Tilling Group neighbour, Thames Valley, to form the Thames Valley & Aldershot Omnibus Co Ltd, with the fleet name Alder Valley. The new company briefly used the red colour scheme seen on this 1961 AEC Reliance 2MU3RV with its 43-seat Weymann body in Woking in 1972, before the adoption of NBC poppy red. *Dale Tringham*

ABOVE: The adoption of an all-white livery for NBC's coaches replaced distinctive liveries like Midland Red's red/black coach livery. Looking slightly uneasy in National white is this 1965 BMMO CM6T 44-seater, at Coventry's Pool Meadow bus station on a London service in 1973. *Chris Aston/Omnicolour*

BELOW: Some relatively old BET double-deckers survived to appear in NBC corporate liveries. At St Annes in 1980 is a Ribble 1963 Leyland Titan PD3/5 with a full-fronted Metro-Cammell 72-seat body. The side advert promotes National Express. *Gavin Booth*

ABOVE: From the mid-1970s Northern General buses wore two liveries – NBC poppy red for 'country' buses, running outside the Tyne & Wear PTE area, and yellow for buses operating totally within the PTE area. Here a 1977 Bristol VRTSL6L with a 74-seat Willowbrook body, heading on to the Tyne Bridge for Washington, passes a 1965 Leyland Atlantean PDR1/1 with an Alexander 65-seat body heading into Newcastle. *Gavin Booth*

BELOW: The integral Leyland National quickly became NBC's standard single-deck model, in the absence of any real choice. At Dover in 1978 is a 1976 49-seat East Kent 11351A/1R model. *Gavin Booth*

ABOVE: City of Oxford received Daimler Fleetlines until 1971/72. In Oxford in 1973, wearing a simplified version of the company livery, with Oxford South Midland fleet names, is a 1971 CRG6LX with a two-door Alexander 70-seat body. *Dale Tringham*

BELOW: East Midland continued to buy Bristol RE buses until switching to Leyland Nationals in 1972. This is a 1972 RELL6G with a two-door ECW 44-seat body. Dual-door buses were briefly popular at this time, but most operators reverted to single-door vehicles. *Stewart J. Brown*

ABOVE: South Wales Transport briefly received three AEC Swifts in 1969, 2MP2R models with Marshall 48-seat two-door bodies, but these were transferred to NBC's new London Country company in 1971. Further Swifts intended for South Wales were diverted to London Country. *Royston Morgan*

BELOW: The whole proud tradition of Midland Red largely disappeared under NBC control. Between 1970 and 1974 140 Fords with Plaxton Derwent 45-seat bodies were received, but these had relatively short lives and some were shortened by Midland Red's Carlyle Works to create 27-seat midi-buses. This is a 1972 R1014 45-seater in Coventry in 1977. *Gavin Booth*

ABOVE: Although the Bristol VRT had become NBC's standard double-deck model, there were also batches of Leyland Atlanteans for former BET companies, including some with ECW bodies, as on this 1972 PDR1A/1R with a two-door 72-seat body, seen in Gateshead & District green in 1974. *Stewart J. Brown*

BELOW: Under NBC the larger companies were split up prior to privatisation, including the once-mighty Midland Red. In 1981 the rump of the company, which had lost its services in the West Midlands PTE area in 1973, was divided into four bus-operating companies. The eastern area, based in Leicester, was renamed Midland Fox, and was one of the first companies to introduce minibuses in the mid-1980s. In 1985 a new Ford Transit 190D with a 16-seat Robin Hood body picks up in suburban Leicester. *Gavin Booth*

Appendix | BET IN ABCs

In the days before the Internet, bus enthusiasts relied very much on the printed word for information about the UK's bus fleets. The magazine Buses Illustrated provided fairly up-to-date news, but just as Ian Allan's railway ABCs provided information for thousands of young locospotters in the 1950s and 1960s, the publisher recognised that there was a growing interest in buses and that the ABC principle could be applied in the same way. Young bus enthusiasts armed themselves with any information they could get hold of, and although the first bus ABCs inevitably concentrated on London Transport, there was soon a clamour for information about

bus fleets around the country. At first Ian Allan Publishing identified some of the larger and more charismatic fleets and in the late 1940s and early 1950s produced pocket-size ABCs concentrating on individual fleets. As the interest in buses grew, Ian Allan started producing the regional British Bus Fleets series, though it recognised that there was a major following for some fleets, and in the BET camp Midland Red and Ribble justified their own ABCs right through to the 1960s, while the charismatic south coast fleets – East Kent, Maidstone & District and Southdown – were included in regional ABCs.

These covers show the different graphic styles adopted over the years, and the vehicles chosen for the cover illustrations demonstrate the advance in bus and coach design.

The oldest ABC in this selection is the 1948 Midland Red booklet, illustrating HHA 1, the prototype of the postwar Midland Red double-deck fleet on service to Bewdley. Like so many Ian Allan covers of the time it uses an attractive scraper-board illustration by artist A. N. Wolstenholme. The 1953 Midland Red ABC features another Wolstenholme illustration, of a 1948 C1 coach, BMMO-built with Duple body, on service to London. The 1955 ABC cover shows

one of the AEC Regent double-deckers bought in 1946, and in 1957 another non-BMMO vehicle, one of the 100 all-Leyland Titans bought in 1953, here on the 159 to Coventry. By 1964 Ian Allan had moved to photographic covers, with an Alexander-bodied Daimler Fleetline, again on the 159 to Coventry. The 1965 edition features one of Midland Red's famous BMMO CM5 coaches, on a deserted stretch of the new M1 motorway.

East Kent had its own ABC in 1949, with an attractive cover featuring a fairly new Leyland Tiger PS1 with Park Royal bodywork.